My Flying Boat War

My Flying Boat War

Survival and Success over the Atlantic, Mediterranean and Pacific in WW2

Wing Commander 'Vic' Hodgkinson DFC, RAAF

With Richard Hodgkinson

First published in Great Britain in 2024 by
Air World Books
An imprint of Pen & Sword Books Limited
Yorkshire – Philadelphia

Copyright © Wing Commander Vic Hodgkinson,
DFC, RAAF 2024

ISBN 978 1 39906 561 0

The right of Wing Commander Vic Hodgkinson, DFC, RAAF to be identified as Author of this Work has been asserted by him in accordance with the Copyright, Designs and Patents Act 1988.

A CIP catalogue record for this book is
available from the British Library

All rights reserved. No part of this book may be reproduced or transmitted in any form or by any means, electronic or mechanical including photocopying, recording or by any information storage and retrieval system, without permission from the Publisher in writing.

Typeset by Mac Style
Printed in the UK by CPI Group (UK) Ltd, Croydon, CR0 4YY.

Pen & Sword Books Limited incorporates the imprints of After the Battle, Atlas, Archaeology, Aviation, Discovery, Family History, Fiction, History, Maritime, Military, Military Classics, Politics, Select, Transport, True Crime, Air World, Frontline Publishing, Leo Cooper, Remember When, Seaforth Publishing, The Praetorian Press, Wharncliffe Local History, Wharncliffe Transport, Wharncliffe True Crime and White Owl.

For a complete list of Pen & Sword titles please contact

PEN & SWORD BOOKS LIMITED
47 Church Street, Barnsley, South Yorkshire, S70 2AS, England
E-mail: enquiries@pen-and-sword.co.uk
Website: www.pen-and-sword.co.uk
or
PEN AND SWORD BOOKS
1950 Lawrence Rd, Havertown, PA 19083, USA
E-mail: uspen-and-sword@casematepublishers.com
Website: www.penandswordbooks.com

Flying Officer Vic Hodgkinson in the UK in 1940,
painted by his brother, Corbett Hodgkinson.

This book is dedicated by his family to the memory of Vic Hodgkinson, his mates 'Attie' Wearne and 'Thursty' Thurstun, and the wartime crews of Nos. 10, 20 and 40 Squadrons RAAF.

Contents

Foreword		viii
Introduction		x
Chapter 1	Early Days	1
Chapter 2	Surviving Training	12
Chapter 3	Taking to the Skies	30
Chapter 4	On a Seagull's Wings	41
Chapter 5	Pembroke Dock	62
Chapter 6	Into the Mediterranean	99
Chapter 7	Sunderlands in Scotland	110
Chapter 8	Promotion	126
Chapter 9	Our Ditching on 28 April 1941	131
Chapter 10	In the Operations Room	145
Chapter 11	Encounter with a Condor	154
Chapter 12	Seeking the Enemy	161
Chapter 13	The Flying Cats	172
Chapter 14	Supply Drops	188
Chapter 15	Chief Flying Instructor	203
Chapter 16	From Flying Boat to Boeing 707	223
Appendix: Plymouth Sound Notes		230
Postscript		235
Index		237

Foreword

It gives me great pleasure to write a forward to this book.
I first met Vic Hodgkinson in 1982 when I was Commanding Officer of 424 Southampton Squadron of the Air Training Corps. At the time the Squadron had created and was running a public museum dedicated to the genius R.J. Mitchell and his legendary Spitfire aircraft. Vic was the lead member of the Sandringham Society which had just been successful in returning one of the last four engine flying boats (Beachcomber) to Great Britain, the Sandringham being the civilianised version of the wartime Sunderland, a type with which Vic was so familiar. Vic suggested that if we could re-locate and enlarge the aircraft museum it would be possible to permanently public display this iconic Flying Boat.

This was a huge challenge, but we were successful and opened the new museum in Albert Road South in Southampton complete with the Sandringham Flying Boat in 1984.

In order to do this, we had the enormous task of dismantling the Aircraft where she lay on the shoreline of Southampton Water and then taking her component parts to the new location in Albert Road South for reassembly.

Throughout the operation Vic and his good friend Dick Froggett (ex Flying Boat Engineer) were absolutely inspirational. Vic worked countless hours with the staff and cadets of the Squadron in this engineering task which had probably never been performed outside factory conditions before. Vic seemed to enjoy immensely working with the young, uniformed air minded youth. I believe they reminded him of what he once was.

Once the Sandringham was installed Vic would travel from Lymington to Southampton two or three times a week to work on the aircraft he loved, which must have brought back so many memories to him.

Although at the time I knew a little about Vic's civilian flying career I had almost no knowledge of his distinguished wartime service – the reason being he simply never mentioned it.

The project attracted many aircraft enthusiasts who in Vic's company would often be vocal about their knowledge of aviation and in particular Flying Boat operations, completely unaware of who they were talking to. Being the gentleman, he was Vic would never correct or contradict them if they were wrong, he would simply look at me and put on a wry smile which said everything.

Vic was one of the most unassuming people I have had the pleasure to work with and one who became a good friend. He was a part of that generation who gave freely and asked for very little in return.

I am delighted that at last Vic's distinguished Service record on Flying Boats has been recorded for posterity.

Sqn Ldr Alan Jones MBE CRAeS (Ret'd)

Introduction

My father always wanted to fly. The son of a sign-writer, with one sister and four brothers (Frank and Roy were official Australian war artists), he grew up in Concord, Sydney, Australia on the flight path between Mascot (now Sydney Kingsford-Smith) airport and RAAF Richmond in the days of the pioneering aviators – such men as Charles Kingsford-Smith, Bert Hinkler, Francis Chichester and Amelia Earhart. As a schoolboy he was in the front of the crowds for the opening of the Sydney Harbour Bridge, when a horseman rode out of the crowd, slashed the tape with a sword and disappeared back the way he had come.

Growing up in Lymington, UK, I knew that my father was a pilot for BOAC and that he had flown flying boats for the Royal Australian Air Force in the Second World War. In the attic there were a few dusty mementoes of his RAAF service, including fleece-lined flying boots, a Japanese sword and special flying sunglasses.

My father rarely spoke of his wartime experiences, and it was not until his retirement from BOAC in 1971, when he had accumulated more than 19,300 flying hours, that he began to type, and hand annotate, a record of his remarkable career. I believe that originally there were to have been two parts, covering both his military and civilian flying careers.

During the period my father was compiling his memoirs I purchased my first home computer, together with a scanner and printer and I duly offered to provide him with a version that could be printed, easily updated and shared. Having printed several copies, I gave them to my father, and they remained with him until he passed away in 2010.

In his retirement he spent hundreds of happy hours refurbishing the Short Sandringham flying boat, *Beachcomber*, in Southampton's Solent Sky Museum, contributing to maritime aviation books, expanding his collection of flying boat photographs and books, and corresponding with museums, aviation societies and ex-colleagues all over the world.

During the first Covid lock down and looking for something to fill the hours, I remembered his memoir. Following our father's death, my younger brother, Rod, had scanned many photographs from our father's albums and shared them with both elder brother, Bob, and myself.

So, I set about producing a revised version, correcting spelling errors and duplications, and incorporating photographs with the idea of providing a record for his sons, eight grandchildren and fourteen great grandchildren, and for sharing with the many individuals and aviation organisations that he'd worked with.

He first met our mum in March 1941 when, with his mates, he gate-crashed her twenty-first birthday party in Plymouth. Their paths then parted. He returned, they married in Romford, Essex, in January 1942 and in April they sailed off into the sunset bound for Australia. Continuing his aviation legacy, two of his sons were engineers for British Airways and his two grandsons are both active pilots, for British Airways and the RAF.

The account of his military flying life is contained in this book together with many of his extensive collection of photographs. In compiling this document, I've come to appreciate a number of things … he flew on the front line throughout the war in both hemispheres and survived (which is probably what made him such an optimist, with a great sense of humour). He was always ready to help anyone, never being impressed by military rank alone. He tragically lost many close friends (a number of whom have no known graves) and that, up until their passing, he kept in contact with his mates that he trained and flew with in 1939, in 10 Squadron RAAF – the likes of 'Attie' Wearne, 'Thursty' Thurstun and Ron Gillies.

This book is for all of them.

Richard Hodgkinson,
Chandler's Ford, UK,
March 2022.

Chapter 1

Early Days

I became hooked on aviation whilst at Sydney Tech High School in Australia between 1933 and 1937. Our family house, at Concord, Sydney, was on the route between Mascot (the original Sydney airport) and the RAAF station at Richmond, some forty miles to the northwest. A certain amount of traffic seemed to generate between the two and as our house was near the intersection of the main west and north roads it made an obvious landmark for these early aviators. All the aircraft flew low and slow and could be heard for some time before they passed overhead. It was very seldom one escaped my attention.

The normal types were DH Moths, Avians and the highlight of the show – Kingsford-Smith's Southern Cross Fokker and the Lockheed Altair. The arrival of record breakers from overseas always created intense interest from the public and the media and they were greeted by vast crowds on their arrival at Mascot. These were the days of hero worship. My enthusiasm manifested itself in the form of collecting anything concerning aviation that one could lay hands on, such as newspaper cuttings and the like, as well as making solid wood models. Plans for the latter were non-existent, so one resorted to drawing plans from photographs and the like, hoping that the end product resembled the type selected. Rubber band-driven flying models were never a success.

On leaving High School, as the aviation industry was almost non-existent there was no demand for my inexperience. It seemed to attract an enthusiastic bunch of people who existed from hand to mouth and who had barely enough to live on let alone own an aircraft. The Royal Australian Air Force also ignored my applications. Jobs were scarce, but my father got me employment at the paint factory where he worked as a sign writer in the advertising department. I became a spray and brush painter on display work with British and Australian Lead Manufacturers (BALM), which was a subsidiary of Dupont and ICI.

About this time the Sydney Technical College advertised an Aircraft Construction Course. This was a night school course, and I jumped at this opportunity. It entailed, after leaving work on the appropriate days, cycling three miles home, a clean-up, supper, a walk of half-a-mile to the railway station, a seven-mile trip and another two by tram. I arrived home around 23.00 hours – all this for three nights per week.

There were around a dozen of us enthusiasts and it was rare for anyone to miss a session, which was more than we could say for the instructors. They seldom appeared and we were left to discuss aviation and make DH60 wing ribs, spars, struts and metal fittings. Although I lost touch with most of this group, I discovered many made their mark in general aviation. I was the only one to make a career as a pilot.

After a year or so of this I was offered a job as a storekeeper by the person in charge of the course, Frank Gannon. This aircraft store was a venture by the ship chandlers Paul and Gray of Sydney and was situated in a hangar at Mascot Aerodrome. Stock consisted of nuts and bolts, planks of spruce, a Cardington Ford engine (no doubt for a Flying Flea, which seemed to catch the imagination of the public at the time) and various bits and pieces. There was little turnover of stock, and one wonders how the show existed. My wage dropped 10 shillings from £3 a week and, due to the remoteness of Mascot and the distance, investment in a car was vital.

Of course, I still attended the night school course. Most of my customers were owners of private light aircraft who appeared to be permanently short of cash and on the scrounge for nuts and bolts and the like. Occasional small orders were received from Holymans Airways, who shared this hangar and operated the four-engine D.H.86 Express Airliner on the Melbourne-Sydney-Brisbane route. No doubt they obtained the bulk of their spares from DH, which was established in a hangar nearby.

A couple more years of this, with continuing applications to the RAAF for entry for pilot training or on the ground, resulted in a Trade Test as Storekeeper in 1936. I was advised not to press the choice of Painter for no one had been selected from that mustering for a Sergeant Pilot's course. Neither had anyone been selected from the Stores section, but it was the better of the two. Application for Cadet Pilot Training was a social priority and normally only sons of doctors, solicitors and the like were considered. I was accepted and reported for enlistment in January 1937 at RAAF Richmond.

I was allotted the service number 2665. A motley bunch of thirty-two 'erks' ranging from prospective ground engineers to cookhouse cleaners assembled for the issue of equipment, plus a Lee Enfield rifle and side arms. The next and following days until completion of the course a month later were spent 'Square Bashing'. Housing was in separate blocks of approximately twenty-four rooms (twelve up – twelve down) with ablutions on each floor. Separate rooms were provided and, although small, were comfortable. Of course, every area was kept spotless by the inmates with daily inspections by the Block Corporal and weekly inspections by the Commanding Officer or his representative, generally, the Orderly Officer of the day. Panic Night was Monday, when everyone was

Marching to the hangars.

allotted an area of the block to clean – ablutions, stairs, verandas, surrounding garden area, etc.

The normal assembly parade for raising the flag included marching to the hangar area. Of these, Tuesday's parade was the Station Commander's parade when rifles and side arms were worn and the full procedure of raising the flag was carried out to the accompaniment of the station band, followed by the normal march to work complete with these accoutrements and the band.

Any personal problems were sorted out within the group and the culprit dealt with. Really there was a good spirit amongst the airmen. There was of course the odd incident. We did have a spate of personal soap inadvertently left in the showers being stolen. The culprit was soon discovered when a bar of soap with a razor blade inserted in it was left lying around in the ablutions. One can imagine the result of using such a trap.

Inspection for dust above doors and the like by over-zealous corporals was discouraged by odd airmen inserting a broken razor blade into the woodwork in this area, with a small proportion protruding. Of course, this was placed in an area where the culprit couldn't be identified.

Unless one was detailed for weekend guard or duty storekeeper duties (sometimes cook house duties) one was free to leave the station from falling out parade at 16.30 hours on Fridays to first parade Mondays at 08.30 hours. These duties came around about twice a year, so were no hardship, but one was always pleased when they were completed.

Having indulged in rugby union and athletics – 220 and 440 yards my speciality – I joined the small group which represented the station. This gave me the privilege of finishing work half-an-hour early for training. Some of us keen types carried on after supper with five-mile cross-country training. I also realised that these activities might assist my applications for a Sergeant Pilots course, which was applied for when promulgated at six monthly intervals. I am sure it helped.

The RAAF athletic team at Richmond in 1939. I am second from the left in the back row.

Hawker Demons at Richmond in 1937/8. Flight Lieutenant Braithwaite is standing on the left.

Hawker Demons in the air.

6   My Flying Boat War

The food in the mess was good and it was supplemented by a small amount deducted from our pay as agreed by common consent. To give one an idea of the standard, some Friday lunches included a plate of oysters.

On completion of the Rookies Course, my posting was to the resident No.3 Squadron at RAAF Richmond as a Store Keeper to learn the ropes. I must say that the numerous forms used in transactions I found beyond my comprehension. As well as No.3 Squadron, which flew Hawker Demons, No.22 was also at Richmond flying Avro Ansons, a newly arrived type. Basically, this was designated a Citizens Air Force squadron (similar to the RAF's Auxiliary Air Force squadrons, such as the No.600 (City of London) Squadron Royal Auxiliary Air Force) staffed by RAAF personnel.

Rookies Course at Richmond, January 1937. I am standing sixth from the right in the back row.

An air-to-air shot of Avro Ansons.

Avro Anson A4-22 pictured over Coogee, Sydney.

8   My Flying Boat War

Then came, in order of position along the tarmac, No.2 Aircraft Depot. This unit was responsible for the central stores and the repair and rebuild of damaged aircraft. The final squadron in this line was No. 9, which flew the Supermarine Seagull V amphibian. They, of course, were used as a Fleet Cooperation Aircraft involved with the Royal Australian Navy, as well as a lone seaplane tender, HMAS *Albatross*.

By today's standards, the airfield was small (but larger than Mascot) and the surface was grass. All buildings were of brick, except the hangars, and of recent construction. It was a happy set-up. Having spent a short time with No.3 Squadron, I repeated the same procedure with 22, and 9 before finally finishing up with No.2 Aircraft Depot, where my duties were to run consumable stores with an Aircraft Hand General, the lowest rank, having no qualifications, as my assistant.

As the name implied, our stocks varied from nuts and bolts to materials such as metal and wood used in the repair work on aircraft in the hangar. Some items like soft soap, which arrived in four-gallon tins, were difficult to account for when doled out in small quantities for washing hands etc. When it came to a crisis and contents were low at the end of the day and record of issues was scant, we resorted to adding water to top up. By the following morning the water had

A Seagull V, coded A2-8, under tow.

No.11 Seaplane Conversion Course, 23 October 1939 to 18 December 1939.

been absorbed and the level returned to a reasonable one, but with the contents somewhat thinner. There was of course a limit to this.

Due to the expansion of the RAAF at this time, no doubt due to the thought of imminent war, the issue of some items of clothing was in short supply. Uniforms were the main problem. The bulk of the kit was made at the Commonwealth Clothing factory. This situation was compounded by the change of design of the uniform from the 1918 style of high-necked tunics, breeches and leather leggings for non-commissioned ranks to the uniforms worn today. So virtually all serving, as well as new intake airmen, required new uniforms.

My issue of these articles did not materialise for eighteen months. This had its advantage for those with uniforms were detailed for parades on special functions in the city. As these were not popular, we refused uniforms as not fitting. The normal issue was two uniforms, a couple of shirts, two pairs of boots, cap, beret, tie, two each of short sleeved singlets and long johns (extremely prickly), two blankets (extra issued in winter), two sheets (changed weekly), and the airman's friend, a 'housewife' which contained sewing gear (thread, needles etc.). On annual CO's inspection of this kit everything had to be laid out in correct order. Any missing items were noted and had to be replaced at the owner's expense and probably a charge laid against the offender.

It was never known for any airman to wear the unsuitable underwear in this warm climate, as it was particularly uncomfortable. An occupant of the room opposite, when asked to produce six of these items, handed over a glass phial of silver fish and moths. Humour was registered with the inspection team, but he still had to provide good replacements.

There were two aircraft in the hangar in front of the store. One was an Anson that had suffered damage when it landed with the undercarriage retracted; the other was a Supermarine Seagull V which had crashed on landing in Jervis Bay, a naval training base to the south of Sydney. They remained there for the duration of my stint in this store. This Seagull, A2-4, was the second last aircraft I flew

Seagull Vs in the air, A2-16 nearest the camera with A2-17 just beyond.

An aerial view of No.1 FTS, Point Cook.

in the RAAF in May 1946 and is currently on display in the RAF Museum, Hendon. Few of these versatile amphibians survive; another is in the Fleet Air Arm Museum at Yeovilton. There is also one of museum standard at Point Cook Australia, having been recovered from the Antarctic.

My constant applications for pilot training bore fruit in my final interview of 1938, when the board told me that I should have been selected for the July 1938 course as a Trainee Sergeant Pilot and would be on the January 1939 intake. I had made it at long last.

All my airman's gear was returned before the Christmas break. Together with two of my also successful friends, on 15 January 1939 I boarded the train for Melbourne and Point Cook, the Flying Training School of the RAAF.

Chapter 2

Surviving Training

The rules were changed over the Christmas period and as a result no Sergeant Pilots courses were scheduled. Consequently, we found ourselves listed as 'cadets'.

We were the first of this scheme and probably the last. The course schedule was for six months as a Junior and the remaining six as senior cadets. It contained the normal procedures of flying – the theory of flying, maths, meteorology, navigation, engines, airframes, law, armament, drill, service history, parachutes and so on. We were accommodated in barrack blocks containing approximately twenty cadets each. There were separate rooms on two floors each containing

The members of No.25 Cadet Course pictured at Point Cook in January 1939. In the back row, from left to right, are the following cadets: Trigg, Ohlmeyer, Judell, Sargeant, Williams, Saunders, Gomon, Bracegirdle, Arnold, O'Brien, Newstead, Ring, Coventry, and Gamble. In the middle are, again left to right: Gordon, Turnbull, Knowles, Springbett, Black, McMahon, Willard, Miles, Sullivan, Kessy, Thurstun, Thompson, and Palmer. The front row, meanwhile, comprises the following: Marks, Pfeiffer, Yoeman, Vernon, Alexander, Wearne, Stevenson, May, Hodgkinson, Nichols, Conaghan, Kirkman, and Cox.

ablutions. There were five such buildings, with an annex for the overflow. Course cadets were allocated in the order of senior cadet, junior cadet alternatively throughout the buildings. A separate building on this quadrangle arrangement provided the mess and anti-room facilities.

There were four flight divisions. The two senior flights were denoted as A and B and the junior course as C and D. A and C flights occupied one side of the quadrangle, B and D the other. Those in the annex were divided between the two. There were fifty in our intake and approximately the same amongst the Seniors, give or take those few Seniors who had not completed the distance for some reason or another.

Within hours of arrival the Seniors called a meeting. During this they read out the riot act and threatened us with punishments for misdemeanours and anything they considered didn't please them – and as we soon discovered, these were unlimited. Life became almost unbearable for the next six months.

The first day was filled in being measured for uniforms, flying helmets and flying goggles (yes, made to measure), cap, flying gloves complete with inner silk

Machine-gun training.

Parachute training gets underway, with our feet firmly planted on the ground.

Supermarine Southampton and trainee parachutists at Point Cook.

"Live" parachute practice!

A Supermarine Southampton at Point Cook – last flown approximately October 1939.

liners, speaking tubes, overalls, and the like. To dress in the mess in the evening while awaiting our uniforms to be made, we had to source a dinner suit, shirt and tie-able bow tie. Until such time as our uniforms appeared, at breakfast we were permitted to appear in clean overalls wearing a tie.

We were also issued with light flying overalls, plus a parachute. This was stowed together with the other flying gear in a personal lockable locker in a hangar. Parachutes were recalled periodically for inspection and repacking and a serviceable one issued to replace it. Parachutes had a further benefit apart from the safety factor. It was a strict rule that cadets had to be at the double (i.e., run) when not carrying a parachute on the tarmac. We soon found the value of this order and made sure that if for any reason we had to cover this area, we carried our parachutes, flying or not.

The first evening, after supper, all Hell was let loose. All fifty of us were lined up by some of the Seniors and marched the mile to the hangar area where we were ordered to strip off (stark naked) and climb over one of the high aircraft ladders, assisted by a powerful jet of water from a fire hose up our back sides. That completed, it was down on all fours to push peanuts with our noses across the concrete tarmac. Next was to double along the slipway/pier to jump from a height into the sea. One of our number refused, but was thrown in. He called for help as a non-swimmer and a couple of the Seniors jumped in to save him. Amongst ourselves, we found that he was an excellent swimmer.

This, then, was our initiation. But from then on, the pressure continued until the posting of this bunch, six months later. I must say that it was a minority of Seniors who inflicted the worst punishments. There were a number who were nice blokes, but they were bound to support their members and, therefore, we had no recourse to them or higher authority. If we did, then we were afraid that it may be taken as a sign of not conforming and lead to our dismissal. So, the only course left open was to suffer these indignities, hoping things would ease up and try to survive the course. We were over a barrel.

So, the Seniors had complete control over us, with the power to dish out extra drills, require us to do all their chores – polish their shoes, keep their rifle and side arms clean, clean and polish their rooms, run errands, serve tea etc. – and anything that came into their fertile brains. We were hounded from morn to well after lights out, and all the time over weekends when leave wasn't granted.

Normally weekend leave occurred once a month, but there were times when it was two months between breaks. Extra drills could be imposed by any senior and the Warrant Officer Drill Instructor. The victim(s) were required to be kitted out with full pack, rifle and sidearm and spend the half-hour hour tea break, and after our return to quarters, doubling around the sports oval supervised by a Senior. It was hard going.

Other punishments and 'entertainments' included the following:

- Raids on our rooms, when we were tipped out of bed, all bedding thrown out onto the gardens, and drawers tipped out.
- Juniors ordered to form up in the Quadrangle for inspection (stark naked). At one time an electric shock gadget was produced and connected to our private parts. Other times ordered into a large lily pond to catch frogs.
- Sent out to the bombing range to bring back the remains of practice bombs. We got over that one for a while when we collected a supply at weekends and planted them in a cache. We could then, when ordered to bring one back, spend a reasonable time out there in the darkness away from this bedlam. They soon tumbled to our antics and marked specific items, which we had to produce.
- Ordering people up trees where one could remain for hours.

There appeared to be no limit to the variety of these punishments. It was common for water fights to be ordered between blocks, using buckets and fire hoses. This mess had to be cleaned up before inspection the following morning. Occasionally these fights were ordered after the quarters had been prepared on the Monday Panic Night and all our efforts done for naught. All had to be made good by the juniors.

18   My Flying Boat War

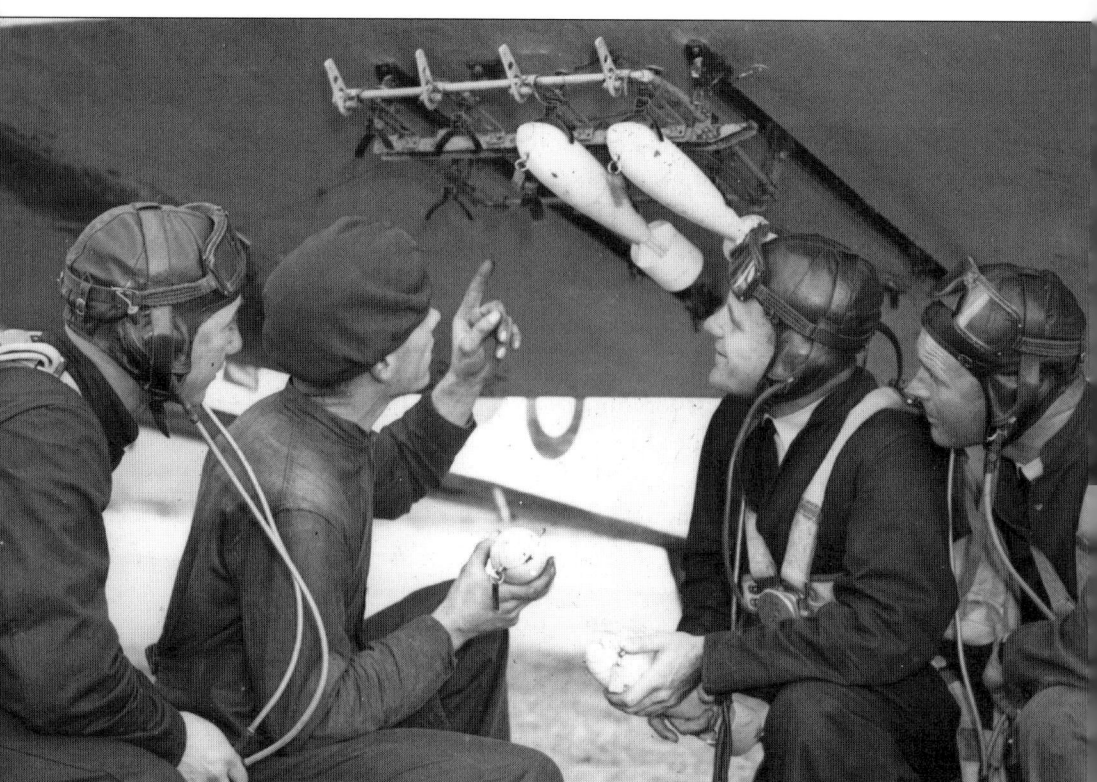

Bombing instructions.

We, as juniors, were allocated, in teams of two, to sections of our block and we were responsible for keeping these clean and tidy at all times. One group the stairs, another the verandas, etc. For some reason, we had to provide all the cleaning polishes, cloths and so on. The verandas, for instance, which were exposed to the elements, were polished to mirror finish. The shower trays, taps, and all of the brass fittings also required this standard.

Rooms of course were the individual's responsibility and required the same treatment. Beds, bedding, and clothing had to be laid out all ship-shape. Dust or any breach of the rules meant an extra drill. It was extremely difficult to please our superiors and at times we were marked down for punishment whether we deserved it or not. As mentioned, the Seniors' rooms, shoes, rifles etc., were also on this list.

The official routine for each working day was as follows:

- Reveille and PT. (06.00 hours).
- Return to barracks – shower, dress for breakfast, prepare room and block for inspection.

- Breakfast – complete block, room cleaning etc.
- On parade for drill session.
- Return rifle and side arm to room.
- Fall in for march to hangar/classroom area (one mile).
- As rostered – flying or ground subjects.
- Fall in for march back to barracks for lunch.
- Fall in for march back to hangar area for flying or ground subject.
- Fall in to march back to barracks for afternoon tea. Serve Seniors, or extra drill.
- Five-mile cross-country run. On return sport or repeat the five miles.
- Return barracks – dress for dinner.
- Report in mess for inspection.
- Dinner.
- Juniors W/T practice and instruction.
- Study period.
- Free period.
- Lights out.

Square Bashing (drill) was to a high standard and thumped into us by the Warrant Officer who seemed to have acquired the sadistic habits of our Seniors. Haircuts could often be ordered three times a week – he never appeared satisfied with our standards of cleanliness of uniforms, rifles and the like.

Our uniforms were dark blue and, as a consequence, showed the smallest piece of fluff. We all armed ourselves with a small clothes brush and it was a common sight before falling in for small groups to form up brushing each other. He also took great pleasure after a session to order: 'For inspection – present butts'. As the surface of the parade ground was gravel – which became muddy after rain – we couldn't avoid his scorn and the extra drill imposed. There was no love lost and he firmly fitted into the enemy bracket. I guess most drill instructors are born with this streak, and he was no exception. One suspects that he was also getting a rake-off from the station barber.

All movements outside the barracks area were strictly 'To attention'. That is in marching order, whether in groups or alone. Someone seemed to be always watching to report slackness.

Flying and ground subjects were alternated each week. One week, Juniors would fly in the mornings with class lessons in the afternoon, while the following week courses would carry out the reverse procedure. Ground subjects covered meteorology, engines, airframes, navigation, maths, armament, parachutes, photography, theory of flight and Air Force law, this latter subject by a lawyer, a great character, who related many spicy court cases. His was the last slot in the

An excellent side profile of Westland Wapiti A5-37.

Westland Wapiti and cadets.

The cockpit of a Westland Wapiti.

week's work. It was difficult to remain awake during class work, especially in the afternoons, and it was quite common for the bulk of the class to drop off. Lecturers were tolerant for they no doubt knew of our enforced nocturnal escapades.

On the flying side, the Junior course was split into DH60 (Moth) and Avro Tutor flights. The Senior course all flew the Westland Wapiti. For my sins, the Avro became my problem. I found it extremely difficult to master its characteristics. It was light on the controls and appeared unstable, no doubt due to my tense approach and over corrections. Instructors were changed, but the problem persisted. The inevitable came when the Chief Flying Instructor gave me a Scrub Test. Somehow, he thought it was worth persevering and my final assessment read 'Below average – under confident'. One couldn't get any lower than that!

The sequence of instruction was:

- Passenger flight.
- Taxying and handling engine.
- Effect of controls.
- Further effect of controls.
- Straight and level flying.
- Stalling, climbing and gliding.
- Taking off into wind.
- Medium turns with and without engine.
- Approaches and landings.
- Spinning.
- First solo.
- Low flying.
- Climbing turns.
- Steep turns with and without engine.
- Side slipping.
- Action in the event of fire.
- Forced landings.
- Instrument flying.
- Landing with engine.
- Taking off and landing cross wind.
- Aerobatics.
- Night flying.
- Cross-country flying.

As on all flights in RAAF aircraft, glide landings were carried out in daylight – right up to my Sunderland and Catalina days. It was good practice for forced landings and no doubt this was its object.

My first solo was achieved after 14.05 hours. This, of course, included all the pre-solo items listed above, many of which are not required in today's civil requirements. However, my performance left a lot to be desired. A total of 61.30 hours was the total logged, including thirty minutes dual and fifteen minutes solo night flying.

There was only one incident I can recall at this time, and that concerned one of our members in 'B' Flight – those on the DH 60s. It was impressed on us that in the case of an engine cut on take-off the procedure was to land ahead. Never turn back. Well, this chap, Gordon by name, did have an engine failure at around 500 feet and turned back to make a successful landing. Luckily there was no wind. We never knew what the powers that be said, but he completed

Surviving Training 23

The dangers of training – the wreckage of a Gipsy Moth and Avro Tutor at Point Cook, approximately 1938.

Another type used in RAAF training – an Avro 643 Cadet. This particular example, A6-20, was built by A.V. Roe & Co at Newton Heath, Manchester, in January 1938. Arriving in Australia in March the same year, it remained in RAAF service until 1944. Note the cover over the rear cockpit.

Cadet Training Unit, Point Cook, 1939. The aircraft seen here include DH 60s, Avro Tutors and Westland Wapitis.

A Miles Magister, possibly at Point Cook. With the serial number A15-1, this was sole example of this type that was acquired by the RAAF.

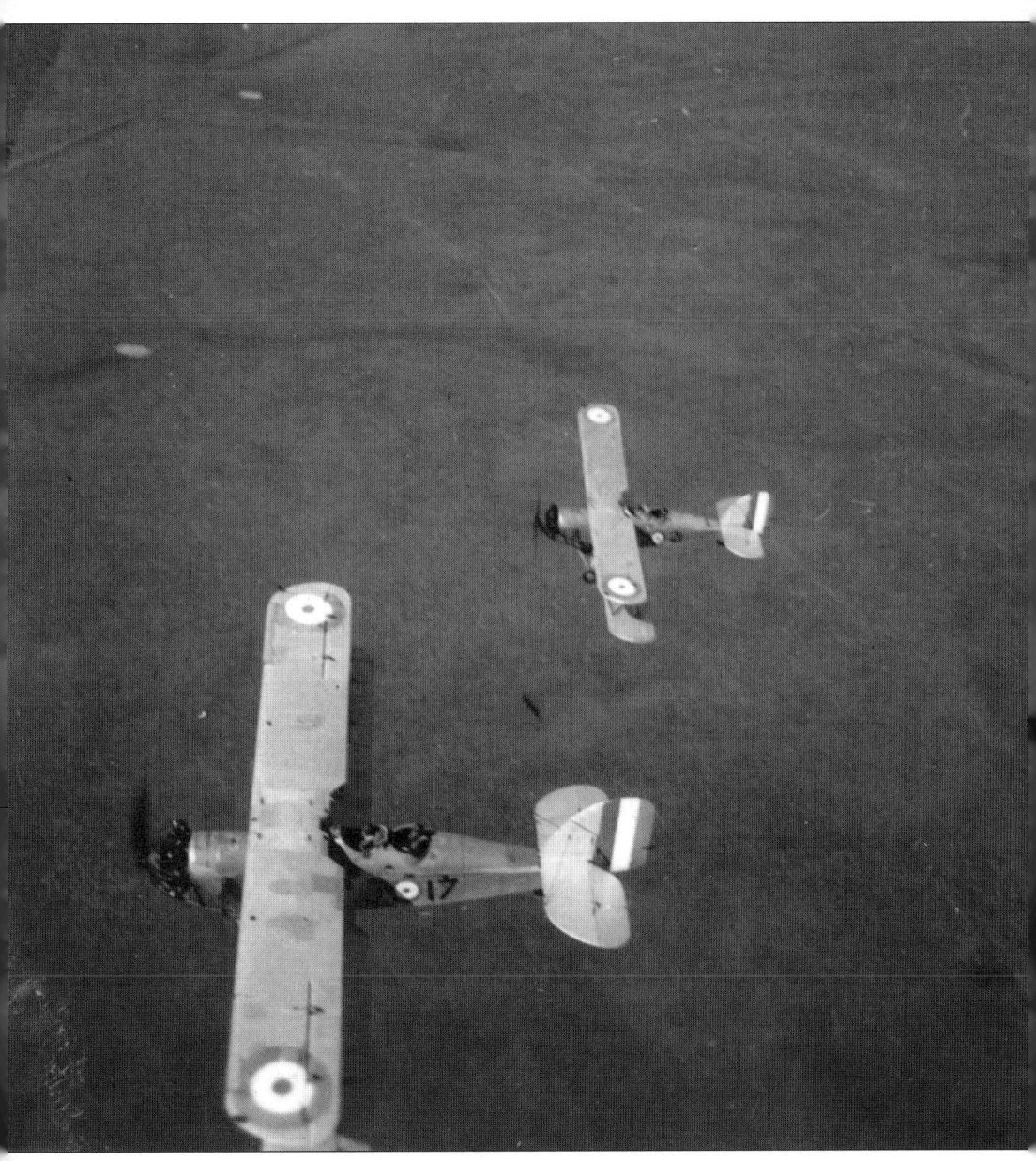

A pair of Westland Wapitis flying over the Australian countryside.

the course. He was known as 'Flash' Gordon from then on. He had another incident on Wapitis later on – but more of that in due course.

The attendance of the weekly station cinema and church parades on Sundays was compulsory, like all things. Objections to attend either received the punishment of digging a hole and filling it in during this time. One got the message. As there was no provision for cadets of the Catholic faith on the station, they were bussed to the church at the adjoining town of Laverton. This proved a lifesaver.

Due to our enforced activities, our appetite for food was a problem. The food provided by the mess was more than adequate for a normal person, but in the evenings our systems demanded topping up. The station canteen stocked sweets, chocolate, biscuits etc. and long queues were common, the Seniors taking precedence in the line. Our staple diet after hours was bread, jam, cocoa, sugar and condensed milk. Butter wouldn't keep due to the warm temperatures.

By the end of the week bread became very stale, but, coated with jam, it allayed the pangs; anything edible was welcome in our state of hunger. As these items were not stocked by the canteen and our confinement to the station was for weeks on end, our supply was obtained by the Roman Catholic contingent each Sunday, from the store at Laverton. Alcohol consumption was restricted to one bottle of beer a week. As I didn't drive at that period, there was no problem.

The anti-room was divided, with Juniors confined to one side – the dividing line being marked by a settee. It was forbidden to enter the sacred Senior area except on command of the opposition, and when on this sacred ground Juniors had to double and keep doubling until commanded by the Seniors to 'halt'. Normally the Seniors asked silly questions, and occasionally ones on aircraft. Ignorance resulted in penalties.

On assembly for dinner, the course was lined up for the inspection of uniform cleanliness, clean shirts, fresh handkerchief, shoes polished. As mentioned already, before uniforms were issued dinner suits and bow ties were worn (the latter had to be correctly tied), fingernails inspected and everything to their satisfaction. As usual penalties were allocated. This completed, the order was given 'sheeps and dogs, Juniors'. We split up into two groups of dogs and sheep, got down on all fours with the sheep leading, proceeded around the mess floor barking and baaing.

We proceeded into the Mess Room which was laid out with three long tables, two parallel and the other across the top end for the officers, of whom there were normally two, the two under officers, four cadet sergeants and the odd Senior. The order of seating on the other tables was Senior and Junior alternatively. So, we were hemmed in by this lot. There appeared to be no respite from them.

Table manners were strict, and protocol always observed. Seniors were served first. Often, we were ordered to perform a 'square meal'. On command, the procedure was for all Juniors at that table to place food on their fork. The Junior at the top became The Right Fugleman (in military terms the one at either end of a squad – Right or Left Fugleman) whose actions are followed by the rest of the group, e.g. fixing or unfixing bayonets. He would raise his right hand when ready, and when dropped all moved the fork in the left hand at arm's length, then vertically to the level of one's mouth, then into the mouth. It remained there until the command 'recharge', when the reverse procedure was carried out. It took an awful long time to finish a course. Vegetables always included mashed turnips (known as floor polish and tasted the same) and, despite our hunger, very seldom consumed. The stewards were not permitted to remove these piled up dishes. The contents left over were ordered to be consumed by us at the end of the meal. Occasionally the tables were turned.

Afternoon tea was avoided as it meant serving the Seniors and suffering yet more of their unpleasantness. To achieve this, we made ourselves scarce by hiding under beds or disappearing into bushes. Some of us were, of course, eventually caught for this chore.

One of our number had a sister who was a nurse in Sydney, and she sent a batch of an aperient. The Seniors' tea was suitably laced with this concoction. It put the whole Senior course on the loo for the better part of the week. The medicos never found the reason why, albeit noting that it was only the Seniors who had caught a bug and not us. They never did discover the truth.

At one time during the summer there was a plague of rather smelly moths. They were everywhere. Our doors and windows were fitted with screens to deter insects and the like. During the interval of the weekly cinema show a couple of us managed to return to the barracks to open the doors of the particularly obnoxious Seniors and turn on the lights. We made a point of returning to the barracks before the Seniors to switch off the lights and close these doors.

Each room was full of these foul-smelling insects. There was Hell to pay, and of course we were made to clean up the mess. Nevertheless, it was some small compensation for our treatment.

Towards the end of this course, we decided it was about time the Seniors eased up. So, an approach was made to the under officers on this matter, also pointing out that within six months, as officers, we would be living on equal terms and hopefully friends. Some hope! They blew their top and the next day all Juniors were lined up for the daily cross-country run; but this turned out to be a little different. It had been raining for the past week and the ground muddy with pools of water. As you can imagine our physical fitness was good. We were doubled about fifty yards forward, did around half a dozen body presses, with the Seniors, who supervised us, pushing our faces down into the mud, then run back for a short distance for more press-ups, forward again and so on. This was repeated for most of the course. One can imagine the suppressed resentment from us.

Time was running out for our appearance in the mess for dinner when these Seniors departed in the general direction, no doubt expecting us to follow suit.

Self as a Cadet Sergeant.

We held a meeting on the spot and decided enough was enough and walked back to barracks, cleaned up, met outside the mess and moved in en masse. We were about half an hour late into the mess and I (for some reason) was called over to the Seniors, side to account to the officers the reason for this breech of discipline. I gave reasons, as above, adding that we had not been allowed sufficient time to return for a clean-up to appear at the appointed time.

The officers seemed to accept this, and nothing further was heard from this direction. However, the Seniors called a parade after supper and suggested that if we continued to do their chores and get back into line (i.e., back to square one) they would allow us to give them the traditional end of course party. Naturally we refused and for the final weeks of this course we went our separate ways. Due to circumstances, I seldom met any of these people in my service life, nor many of those stalwarts from my comrades on our course. We became closely knit due to our privations over those six months. The Seniors went their way to their designated squadrons and we for a well-earned couple of weeks' vacation. A couple of our intake disappeared about this time through failing the course.

This was a difficult period for us and although time was listed for study, we never achieved this due to the antics of the Seniors. But we were extremely fit. On return as Seniors my old friend of these days, and subsequently in service and civilian life, 'Attie' Wearne and I found ourselves promoted to Cadet Sergeants in charge of 'A' Flight and 'B' Flight respectively. Why I was chosen has been a puzzle to me ever since. This promotion was the first and probably the only time an airman-orientated cadet had achieved this rank.

A week later the next intake of Juniors arrived, and we were further promoted to Cadet Under-Officers, with four of our course to Cadet Sergeants. Between us it was felt that something had to be done about the system inflicted on us. It was agreed to abolish the sadistic punishments, albeit retaining those necessary for discipline, and also to honour the allocated study period. These intentions came to naught for they disappeared within a short time and we knew not where they went. One feels that the war had upset these peacetime routines and headquarters were considering further training to be done at other bases and not as a cadet scheme. On reflection I guess it was the start of the Empire Air Training Scheme.

Chapter 3

Taking to the Skies

With that out of the way we settled down to a quieter life. My training on the Wapiti commenced on 18 July 1939, and after 2.15 hours dual I became solo. I found the Wapiti a gentle old beast where one could be on the ham-fisted side. It was very forgiving. We became the best of friends as I felt at home when flying it. This was indicated in my final assessment of 'above average no outstanding points'.

Instruction and solo covered all of the above programme, excluding any aerobatics of the spin and roll nature, but included three cross-country flights,

Three flights of Westland Wapitis in formation.

Filling practice bombs.

gunnery, bombing and formation flying on the Wapiti. The bombing targets were on the range north of the field, the gunnery in the sea off Point Cook. The approach to this target was from the land, no doubt to prevent any misaimed shots spraying the station. The aircraft was equipped with a single Vickers machine-gun firing forward through the prop; it was mounted on the port side of the fuselage by the front, pilot's cockpit. Mine developed stoppages and this was cured by the instructor climbing out of the rear cockpit along the side of the aircraft and, hanging on to the edge of cockpit with one hand, clearing the stoppage with the other before returning to his perch.

My first cross-country flight in a Wapiti, to Bendigo and back, occurred on 29 August 1939. It was made with my sergeant instructor firmly tucked down in the open gun position aft. I set course and on reaching height, probably a couple of thousand feet, a wind check was made and a corrected course set. Wind finding procedure was to fly timed courses from a fixed point on the ground, the first forty-five degrees to the original course to the right for a fixed time, then forty-five degrees to the left for the same time, then head direct to the original point, timing this distance. The course back was the wind direction and the time back on this heading was selected on the appropriate tables contained in a small booklet which, I think, was called *Browns Tables for Navigation*, under the appropriate airspeed. This gave the wind speed. The aircraft was flown at 'airspeed'. All a little primitive, but it served the purpose in the days when 100 mph and under was considered the norm. The distance to Bendigo was around 100 miles.

About half an hour later I realised that I had been increasing the throttle continuously. My conclusion was that the throttle lock was not working correctly. During this time, my primary interest was navigation and, this being my initiation to this art, I was working overtime. Came the time when full throttle had come to the forward limit and the old beast would not maintain altitude, so we were on the way down. Sufficient revs were indicated on the RPM gauge.

My instructor was informed – he had his head down studying an 'adult' magazine. His reaction was to climb over the side, reach into my cockpit to operate my throttle and check the RPM indicator. It functioned correctly, so back to his perch he headed where he took control. On looking over the side the twin exhausts were pouring out thick black smoke. The view aft was blanked out by our emissions. It was a cloudless sky apart from our contribution. There was only one way to go and that was down.

The country below was bush, with only one small field of dubious content. It was a full glide approach to this restricted site, and we lobbed in so close to the end of the barbed-wire-fenced field that we caught the fence on the tail skid.

The landing run terminated in some boggy ground. Luckily, we didn't nose over. My instructor then climbed overboard, instructing me to keep the engine running. After a visual inspection and a couple of bursts of power, he gave a signal to cut the engine. The engine stopped, but the enormous thirteen-foot wooden propeller remained turning. The reduction gear had 'stripped' (all the teeth sheared). I dismounted, shedding the Navigation Calculator (CSC), which was strung around my neck, and when the prop had completed its gyrations secured it to a section of the engine with the string from my CSC.

Although there had been no signs of habitation on our way down, people appeared on horses, cars and the like in short time. Some brought hampers and the rest of my short stay was occupied showing these hospitable people the 'intricacies' of the beast, accompanied by a feast of cakes and tea. The instructor meanwhile had commandeered a car to make his way to the nearest telephone to inform base of the problem. Help arrived about an hour later in the form of another Wapiti complete with a couple of fitters. We climbed into the rear cockpit and returned to base.

As mentioned, this field was very small with a bog area at the upwind area. There was a clump of large Gum trees ahead, which presented (to me) a formidable obstacle. However, there was a limited gap in this lot and after becoming airborne the pilot manoeuvred the aircraft to a vertical attitude to pass safely through. A great piece of flying.

Two of the Wapiti had fixed angle undercarriages – an axle to which both landing wheels were attached. The other was known as the split axle type, where separate axles were attached to each undercarriage leg. The fixed type had wheels fitted with high-pressure thin tyres, which didn't have much flexibility and consequently more difficult to control on landing. The other aircraft were fitted with the split undercarriage and the tyres were of the 'doughnut' type, i.e. of larger section. This type was more flexible and forgiving to the rough surface and our 'arrivals'. The Wapiti of our forced landing was of the fixed angle type,

Another view of Westland Wapiti and cadets.

An air-to-air shot I took of a Westland Wapiti, in this case A5-34.

and we were fortunate our landing run stopped before entering the worst of the boggy area otherwise it may have nosed over, causing damage. The retrieving aircraft was of the split angle variety.

Another item of interest was the tail skid arrangement. To compensate for the removal of operational gear, an enormous steel plate took the place of the normal shoe. Also, a tubular bar was fitted through the aft fuselage, protruding out each side. To this was fitted circular lead weights to compensate for the instructor, when not carried.

Although this cross-country only lasted for under an hour, I note that my logbook shows 'X Country Incomplete' with an official time of three hours. This one was not re-run.

My final cross-country, on 2 October 1939, was similarly not without its problems. The detail was to fly a triangular pattern to Deniliquin (180 miles) solo, land, pick up an instructor for the Albury sector (100 miles), where he disembarked, and proceed direct back to base (100 miles).

Everything went well for the first sector. After settling down on course on the next sector my instructor asked where I thought I was going. On checking I found my course was the reciprocal to that expected. He asked for my map to check position, which unfortunately I passed back over the top and not inside. The shattering result was that the slipstream took possession of the map and to my horror it was last seen floating serenely to earth.

Fortunately, the instructor was sympathetic, adding a 'Don't worry, I will get you there'. I am sure he didn't pass on my 'boob', and I was extremely grateful for this.

On arrival another map was produced, and the course was set to base. This sector was easy, for one had only to follow the main line railway to Melbourne, with Point Cook visible from there. My log shows 2.05, 1.10 and 1.15 hours for each sector. There must have been a strong tail wind on the final sector.

Passing out parade, October 1939.

Self at 'Wings' presentation by AVM Goble, with Group Captain Lukis, October 1939.

At this point, I note an incident which occurred when passing a Wapiti being run up for an engine check while on my way to my aircraft. I spotted the lack of the mandatory airman draped across the tail to keep the aft end down. The pupil, engrossed with his head inside checking the instruments, was oblivious to this situation. A group of us had now formed nearby and were shouting and waving to draw his attention. The tail by this time was above the horizontal and when he noticed our excitement, realised the situation and chopped the throttle. The back end came down with a thump causing failure of the structure.

The Passing Out parade, including presentation of Wings and Commission, took place on 22 October 1939. Posting notices were also issued. We had completed the course two months earlier than listed because of the war. Flying and working weekends had contributed to this. Our rank was now Pilot Officer, and my Service Number became 463. I had flown a total of 113.30 hours and been given an assessment of 'Above Average'. No outstanding faults – an improvement on my last effort.

No.11 Seaplane Conversion Course, 23 October 1939 to 18 December 1939. Left to right are 'Thursty' Thurstun, 'Attie' Wearne, Self, McMahan.

My posting was to No.11 Seaplane Conversion Course, at Point Cook, which commenced on 23 October 1939. Four of us were selected. Three of us survived and served in the same squadrons or units throughout the war. The other became ill and didn't follow the same pattern. This Seaplane Training unit possessed a DH60 Moth two-float seaplane, two Supermarine Seagull V amphibians and a solitary wooden-hulled Supermarine Southampton flying boat. The latter was a survivor of two of 1925 vintage acquired from the RAF.

No.11 Seaplane Conversion Course, 23 October 1939 to 18 December 1939. This is DH 60 floatplane A7-36.

The Supermarine Southampton that was used by No.11 Seaplane Conversion Course. Left to right are Self, 'Attie' Wearne, and 'Thursty' Thurstun.

Fairey 111D launching.

Chapter 4
On a Seagull's Wings

The Seagull V was an early version of the famous Supermarine Walrus and therefore similar. It soon became obvious that the Squadron Leader I/C was not interested in flying. We had a flying officer instructor as well, but he soon disappeared from the scene after he crashed one of the Seagulls while 'beating up' his nurse girl friend at a nearby hospital. The engine stalled and he crashed into a valley full of Gum trees. This aircraft was a write off and he and the 'erk' passenger spent some time in hospital with back injuries and the like. So, we were stuck with our Commanding Officer.

Seagull V, A2-2. Pictures exist of this aircraft being launched from a catapult on the port side of a Kent-class cruiser circa 1936 or 1937.

His big interest was the Station cinema, where he would spend hours looking at films. His favourite was the Mickey Mouse series. Aside from our rare flying exercises, the bulk of our working day was spent sorting out the poster bills for future shows and marking the dates thereon. Semaphore, Aldis Lamp, knots and splices and sailing the whaler boat occasionally filled in the rest of the time between the rare flights. During the cinema intervals he would give the audience a rundown on the future week's programme. This week he announced the next programme to be 'Man Chases Woman – with two Mickeys'. There was a deathly hush for a few seconds, then loud cheering from the troops. I don't think that he ever realised what he had said.

Flying the DH60 was rather precarious. The airframe appeared on its last legs and sometimes when in the air the bolt holding the two bracing wires on the centre section would pull out. This, to our alarm, allowed the whole top mainplane to move from side to side. Great caution and delicacy were required to land back without it falling apart. During his first briefing on the Seagull, the CO impressed us that it would be the largest and heaviest aircraft we would ever fly. It weighed three-and-a-half tons. He was a bit out on that one – my largest was the Boeing 707 at 140 tons.

A Seagull V during take-off.

The DH60. It was grossly underpowered, especially with its clapped-out Gipsy 1 engine.

One of the Seagull Vs pictured in the entrance to a hangar.

Take-offs from glassy calm conditions were impossible. I recall one morning when our noble squadron leader plus the heaviest member of our group (both totalled around 400lbs) attempted a take-off in such a situation. They disappeared over the horizon of Port Phillip Bay to return sometime later still waterborne – on the step. That was the end of that day's flying.

There was also the problem that anything above a 6-inch chop meant no flying with the delicate beast. It would not have survived.

Our training on the surviving Seagull covered circuits and landings on both land and water, general flying, a height test – up to 10,000 feet. We had never been up that high before and this was to test our judgement on landing from a high altitude and formation flying. As the other Seagull hadn't been replaced there was a problem of an aircraft with which to format.

The solution was to borrow the solitary Tiger Moth, which had joined the DH60 cadet flight. Each of us were soloed on it, to become the chase aircraft. We rotated between aircraft until this detail was completed. The turbulent

A de Havilland Tiger Moth. This RAF example was used during the early months of the war by RAF Coastal Command on anti-submarine patrols. (*The late Wing Commander H.C. Randall DFC, via Historic Military Press*)

conditions made it difficult to format on this lively aircraft. As the Seagull weighed so much, no one can understand our predicament. Like chasing a bee in a bottle was the expression.

There was no assessment for that course, but my hours had increased to a total of 144. Our next posting was to No.10 Squadron, then being formed in the UK with Short Sunderlands.

After some leave had been granted, which lasted from 18 December to 27 December 1939, we duly set off for the UK. My two colleagues, being West Australians, departed Perth by local airline to Darwin, where we linked up on the Qantas 'C' Class flying boat *Carpentaria*, on which I had joined at Sydney.

As we were travelling through a few neutral countries en route, all items which may have identified our Air Force connections were forbidden. We were issued with civilian passports and our kit was packed in trunks to be forwarded by sea.

This service took thirteen days to Poole, UK. The schedule as follows:

27 Dec 1939	Sydney, Rose Bay – Brisbane – Townsville	Nightstop	Quantas *Carpenteria*
28 Dec 1939	Townsville – Karumba – Groote IS – Darwin	Nightstop	
29 Dec 1939	Darwin – Koepang – Bima – Sourabaya	Nightstop	
30 Dec 1939	Sourabaya – Batavia – Singapore	Nightstop	
31 Dec 1939	Singapore – Penang – Bangkok	Nightstop	Imperial Airways *Corio*
1 Jan 1940	Bangkok – Rangoon – Calcutta	Nightstop	
2 Jan 1940	Calcutta – Allahabad – Gwalior – Raj Sammand – Karachi	Nightstop	
3 Jan 1940	Karachi – Sharjah – Bahrein – Basra	Nightstop	
4 Jan 1940	Basra – Baghdad – Galillee – Alexandria	Nightstop	
5 Jan 1940	Alexandria – Mirabella – Athens – Corfu	Nightstop	Imperial Airways
6 Jan 1940	Corfu – Brindisi – Lake Bracciano – Marseilles	Nightstop	
7 Jan 1940	Marseilles – Lake Hourtin (due weather in the UK)	Nightstop	
8 Jan 1940	Hourtin – Poole. To London by coach	Nightstop	

Qantas covered the route to Singapore, from where Imperial Airways continued the service to the UK. Aircraft were again changed at Alexandria, together with the crews. The service was superb throughout. With first class hotels at night stops, it was a real eye opener to us. At most day transit stops we were taken ashore for the hour turnaround. I believe the fare was £100 Australian – the UK £ was on a par then. It was a trip I never forgot.

A Short Empire flying boat at Calshot. Note the camouflage paint scheme.

Loading bombs beneath the wing of a Seagull.

Refuelling Seagull whilst afloat.

Seagull cockpit...very few instruments!

Seagull A2-4 and admirers! I flew this aircraft, which is now in the RAF Museum at Hendon, UK.

Seagull with crew.

Seagull, possibly at Point Cook.

Seagull A2-7 afloat with unknown individuals.

Seagull A2-7 ashore with unknown individuals.

On reporting to the Air Commodore at Australia House in The Strand, London, the morning after our arrival, our orders were to have a uniform made and equip ourselves with the other items. This entailed an enforced stay of a week in London, which we could ill afford. Our pay authority hadn't arrived (and didn't for some weeks later) and our resources amounted to a little over £20 each. Apart from the uniform costs, accommodation for the week was the other main expense.

We survived in a three-bed room at the Strand Palace but could only afford one light meal a day. We were more than pleased to escape this plight when we were posted to RAF Calshot for a heavy flying boat course.

It was the coldest winter in England for many a year, and we couldn't afford gloves or greatcoats – anyway these hopefully were on their way. We had never experienced snow or these icy conditions, so we were none too happy with the situation. On the trip to Calshot, apart from the snow, icicles had formed on power and telephone lines some reaching to the ground with a number collapsed due to the weight of the ice. Our trip there in the back of an open RAF lorry didn't improve our sense of humour. The water system in the mess was frozen including the toilets.

The mess was about a mile from the hangar area and we three ran the return trip twice a day through the snow to keep warm. One evening the Commanding Officer asked us to a cocktail party where two of his attractive daughters were in attendance. I guess we were a novelty. One said, 'You Australians are a tough lot'. On enquiring 'Why?' she said, 'You never see our officers running without greatcoats to the hangars each day'. I explained that ours were still on the way over and so had none.

A whip around the RAF officers produced some Burberry light raincoats, which made life a little more bearable, but we continued the sprint to the hangars. An issue of greasy overalls was made to cover our uniforms while flying and doing the other chores on the aircraft.

The first of the course aircraft were examples of the Supermarine Scapa, a twin-engine Rolls-Royce Kestrel-powered biplane. Their bottoms were coated with weed some twelve inches long and the engines clapped out. These were for taxying and mooring practice. The other aircraft was a Short Singapore III of 1933 vintage. It was fitted with four Rolls-Royce Kestrel engines, these being positioned between the massive mainplanes in tandem, with two pulling and two pushing. It was cumbersome and far from reliable by the time we got our hands on it.

The Scapas, being obsolete and consigned to taxying, were badly maintained, especially the engines which proved difficult to start, and when they did, emitted quantities of black smoke accompanied by loud knocking noises. Attempts to fly them – some hope with aircraft in this condition – were strictly forbidden. No doubt they filled their role in the programme by saving hours on the Singapores.

The ferrying of crews from flying boats to shore was always a bone of contention at all flying boat bases. The Marine Section crews, especially on cold days, seemed loath to notice our Aldis signals for transport back to the shore. Pickups of crews returning from operation, or Ops, were organised by the Operations Room and these couldn't be ignored.

The lightly powered dinghies were invariably dirty and oily, being used for aircraft maintenance as well, and mostly overcrowded. To avoid damage to our uniforms we remained standing. They were generally wet by spray, as these craft were open with a dodger (canvas screen) fitted to the larger craft. A good sense of balance was required, and it was not unknown for one to capsize.

One day after a taxying detail we were stuck at moorings, around lunchtime, frantically signalling by Aldis for a pickup. Another crew on an adjoining buoy

A Saro Lerwick flying boat. This particular example, L2753 coded WQ-F, crashed while attempting to land off Lismore Island, near Oban, in poor visibility. Only two of the crew survived.

A Short Singapore I photographed at Pembroke Dock.

A Short Singapore taking-off.

were doing the same. These moorings were at the far western end of the Trots (groups of moorings) situated roughly close to where the Fawley Oil Refinery is today and about a mile from Calshot. We were desperate, for if we missed lunch there was no way of organising another one. So, as a last resort someone on the other aircraft fired a red Very cartridge.

This shot to the sky landing on the next Scapa, setting it alight. This brought an instant response from the Marine Section and the fire boat crew who concentrated on this conflagration. Despite their efforts it burnt to the waterline. Our plight was ignored until things had calmed down. So, no lunch that day for us.

On the Singapore side, our training, apart from dual and the odd solo, was to slip moorings, moor up and start the engines. All were extremely cold and wet operations, especially starting. We students took it in turns. The number of pupils on each flight varied from two to seven. The engine start-up procedure was for those detailed to climb out onto the hull, insert the crank handle through the appropriate hole in the engine cowling, operate the priming pump, then crank the selected leading engine until it started. The forward engines were started first and moorings not slipped until both had fired up satisfactorily. It was a direct drive to the engine. Few started first time, so the procedure was repeated until the desired result happened. This was repeated on the other engines in the order required by the pilot, accompanied by the normal hand signals from the pilot.

Firing up of the front engines produced clouds of smoke and the blast of freezing air from the propeller. On moving to the rear engines, one was continuously exposed to this blast, which varied as the pilot altered the throttles for manoeuvring the aircraft. It was far from a pleasant job, more so as we were without warm clothing or gloves. At times, due to reluctant engines, we never moved from the mooring, or when one of both aft engines refused to cooperate spent the period on the water. All engines were required to become airborne. For one week flying was suspended as the aircraft were frozen by sea ice at their moorings.

Night flying was carried out in Guernsey. On 21 February 1940, the flight departed, with three Singapores, to St. Peter Port. There, having squeezed through the manmade harbour entrance, we tied up on prepared moorings.

One of the three Short Singapores entering the harbour at St Peter Port, Guernsey, on 21 February 1940.

Some of the crew on one of the Singapores watch as their aircraft enters the harbour at St Peter Port. A second Singapore can be seen beyond.

Singapore 'M' makes its way to its mooring in the harbour at St Peter Port.

On a Seagull's Wings   57

Singapore 'M' is tied up to a mooring buoy.

The crew of Singapore 'M' disembark into a small boat for the run ashore.

The Short Singapore beached in the harbour at St Peter Port.

The ship that took us home from Guernsey. Within a few months the island would be in German hands.

A Short Singapore at RAF Calshot.

Accommodation was in a hotel nearby. The three kerosene (paraffin) lit buoys were laid in the open sea off the port. The engines persistently broke down and after three days, in which I logged 1.20 hours dual night and 1.50 hours as second pilot on a beat up of Jersey, the whole operation was cancelled due to all aircraft requiring engine changes. They were last seen with beaching gear attached run up on the beach inside the harbour.

The same evening, we were dispatched on the SS *Isle of Sark*, which plied the route between Guernsey and Southampton for return to Calshot. The ship was overcrowded with locals evacuating before the Germans took over. During our short stay in Guernsey, the locals were extremely kind to us. It was also discovered that beer was four pence a glass, champagne cocktails nine pence and Scotch nine pence – by way of example. I had never touched alcohol prior to this, but this changed my ideas.

The course was made up of six RAF pilot officers, one flight lieutenant converting from the Walrus and we three. Up to our arrival back at Calshot and return from Guernsey, our RAF classmates loaned us cash to get by, and, on reporting back, to our relief our trunks had arrived and our pay sorted out. We were solvent once again.

An aerial view of Calshot taken in the 1930s. The presence of Supermarine Southamptons suggests it was not later than 1937. (*Colin van Geffen Collection*)

Sunderlands pictured at Calshot circa 1942 and 1943. In the foreground is Sunderland Mk.III ML819, with, directly behind, a Catalina. (*Colin van Geffen Collection*)

Another aerial view of Calshot, this time circa 1945 or 1946. (*Colin van Geffen Collection*)

At this point, after twenty-one days being frozen to death and twenty-five hours of unproductive flying, we were on our way to the war. The 'Average' assessment appeared in my log, which no doubt all achieved. A complete waste of time.

Chapter 5

Pembroke Dock

Travel to the Squadron, which was based at RAF Pembroke Dock, was by train. We arrived on the evening of 10 March 1940. The station was a blaze of lights, much to our surprise. Apparently, a couple of the airmen were hospitalised with meningitis and the medicos had ordered all windows and doors in the airmen's quarters to be kept open for a week. From this time on our troops and officers were issued with halibut oil pills. To ensure that the troops took the daily dose, the orderly sergeant's duty on first parade each morning was to place a pill in each airman's mouth. They soon became known as 'pink pills for pregnant pilots'. No doubt this was the only part of the UK not blacked out at this time.

The first of three images showing Sunderlands of 210 Squadron pictured off the south coast of England having formed part of the escort for a visit by the French Premier to the UK in 1939.

The Sunderlands of 210 Squadron returning to their base with the south coast in the background. The buildings on the clifftop are of what is today known as Roedean School, which is a few miles to the east of Brighton.

As the mess was full – No.210 Squadron RAF was also in residence – overflow accommodation was provided in the Annex, a large house nearby that had once been occupied by Nelson and Emma. By this time the squadron was near to full strength and had become operational.

A word about its formation. Before the war, the Australian Government had ordered nine Sunderlands, the first ferry crews for the initial three were duly dispatched and completed training with No.210 Squadron RAF at Pembroke Dock (referred to as PD). By this time the war had started, and the Australian Government offered No.10 Squadron RAAF to the RAF for the duration. Maintaining its RAAF designation, the Australian Government was prepared to finance the whole cost. This was duly accepted, and the squadron became operational six weeks from the outbreak of hostilities.

A bit further along the coast, the 210 Squadron Sunderlands are now seen here passing Portslade, a western suburb of the city of Brighton and Hove.

An RAF Short Sunderland, L5803 of 230 Squadron, at Pembroke Dock. Having variously served in Nos. 95, 204, 228 and 230 squadrons, L5803 was struck off charge 22 August 1942.

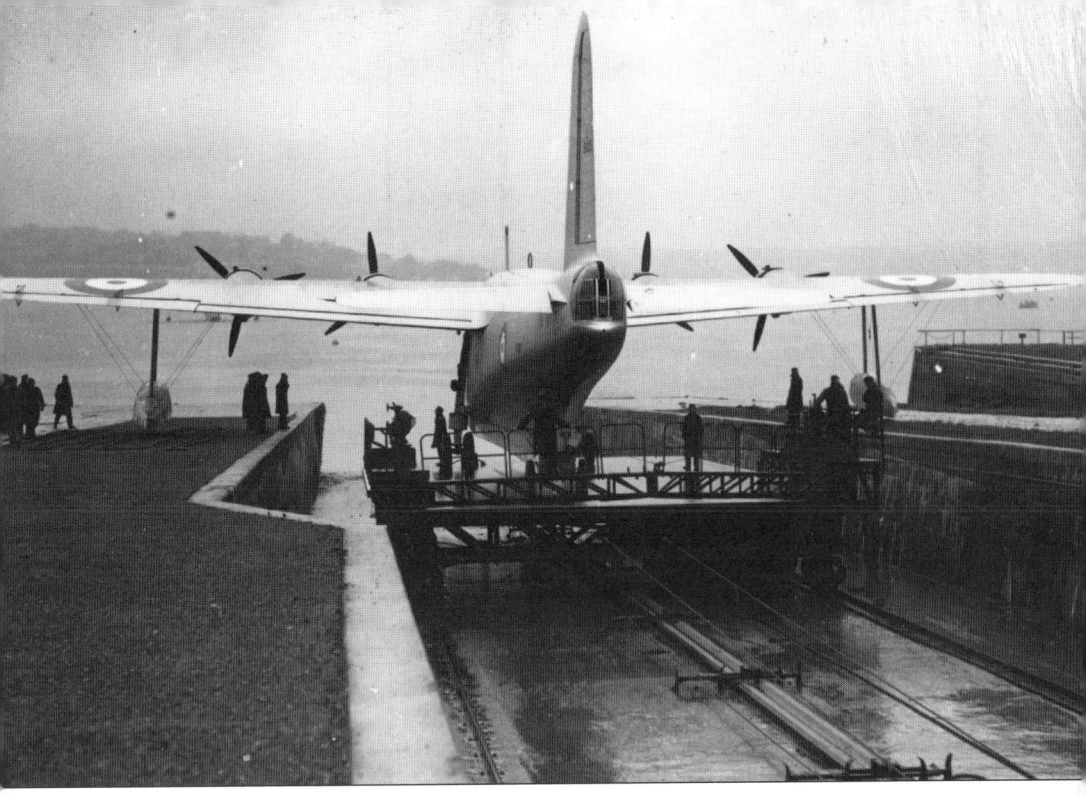

Sunderland L5803 on the trolley while being launched at Pembroke Dock.

Attaching a tow line to L5803 at Pembroke Dock.

66   My Flying Boat War

It is still active in the maritime activities of the RAAF. Also, it was the only permanent Commonwealth squadron to serve in the UK. No.3 (Fighter) Squadron RAAF was its counterpart in the North Africa and Mediterranean area.

The personnel were a mixture of permanent and Citizens Air Force (RAF equivalent RAFVR). There was a severe shortage of second pilots. We numbered

A view of part of the base at Pembroke Dock.

Loading a bomb onto one of our aircraft – possibly at Pembroke Dock.

five for nine aircraft and eight captains, which included the CO and flight commander, who had to cope with administration problems and, therefore, restricted flying. The other crew members were eight Sergeant Navigators and airmen to complete the two Fitter (engineer), one Rigger, one Armourer, two Wireless Operator crew. These latter were mostly of Aircraftsman 1st Class up to the rare corporal, who had passed the Air Gunners' course. There was no provision for airmen aircrew in the RAAF and these airmen were volunteers from the hangar. The minimum rank of RAF aircrew was sergeant, with the appropriate pay.

This lack of sergeant ranks caused problems when some were arrested by the Service police for wearing the Gunner's brevet. Our uniforms were dark blue, and this only added to the confusion. It was not until the influx of men from the Empire Training Scheme, a year or so later, that the RAAF conformed with RAF procedure on this matter. I think these enthusiastic airmen received an additional 6 pence a day for 'dicing with death'. They all were a great bunch.

Self in officers' mess at RAF Pembroke Dock.

Due to the shortage of pilots and navigators we moved from one aircraft to another. The other crew members were allotted their own aircraft and maintained it. Control Officer on flare path duties was also allotted to the second pilots and these were frequent. So, we were very busy boys. Luckily, station duties were not part of our tasks.

Average monthly flying times were around the 100-hour mark and one month I logged 120 hours, day and night. For some reason, no further navigators or pilots were sent from Australia. Around this time the squadron was directed by RAAF HQ, Melbourne that no decorations were to be granted, as issue of these might cause discontent amongst those in Australia who hadn't the opportunity to qualify. It was sometime later that they removed their heads from the sand. The RAF presented DFCs to most of the original captains at the end of their tour, before return to Australia. This may have broken the ice.

In July 1940 the RAF posted three Pilot Officers, two Sergeant Pilots and a couple of navigators to the squadron to relieve the pressure. They were a great bunch and soon fitted into our 'colonial ways' and remained until the arrival of three Flight Lieutenants from Australia, followed by EATS (Empire Air Training Scheme) crew about a year later.

Australian Prime Minister, Sir Robert Menzies, visits 10 Squadron in 1941. It is possible that the location is RAF Mount Batten.

Unlike flying crews of the land-based types, in this squadron each airman crew was responsible for the maintenance of their allotted flying boat. The major jobs (engine changes, airframe damage, complete overhauls etc) were the responsibility of the ground crew. All others, such as refuelling, oil and spark plug changes, gun cleaning, bilging etc., and as well as the cooking, were shared between the aircrew, all of whom normally lived on board. For instance, after a

The original 10 Squadron navigators pictured beside a Sunderland.

patrol, which could last up to ten plus hours, these members changed twenty-three plugs (seventy-two spread between the four engines), greased the exhaust and inlet valves (they were not oil lubricated on the Pegasus, an antiquated piece of equipment), changed the oil when required and certainly topped up, attended to the extractor/engine controls, always a source of trouble, removed and cleaned the guns (salt water spray had to be removed), bombed up, and so.

When this was all completed, tea was brewed on the Primus cooker and perhaps a meal served. Fuel from the over filling of tanks ran into the bilges of the galley, and although the hatches were opened it never ceased to amaze me there was never a serious fire. I believe an RAF Sunderland did 'go up' during a similar event.

The rations issued to aircraft were better than those received in the mess. Occasional steaks appeared, and bacon and eggs as well – probably another incentive for these lads to live aboard.

A damaged 10 Squadron Sunderland being refuelled, by Jerry can, at Alexandria.

Engine maintenance underway on a 40 Squadron Sunderland. Note the platform and supports folded out from the leading edge of the wings.

Another view of the engine maintenance in progress. Don't drop a spanner!

A close-up of the folding maintenance platform on a Sunderland's wing.

A view of a Sunderland cockpit from the inside rear.

My caption to this photograph shows some of 10 Squadron' 'air gunners amidships, Sunderland Mk 1, looking forward'.

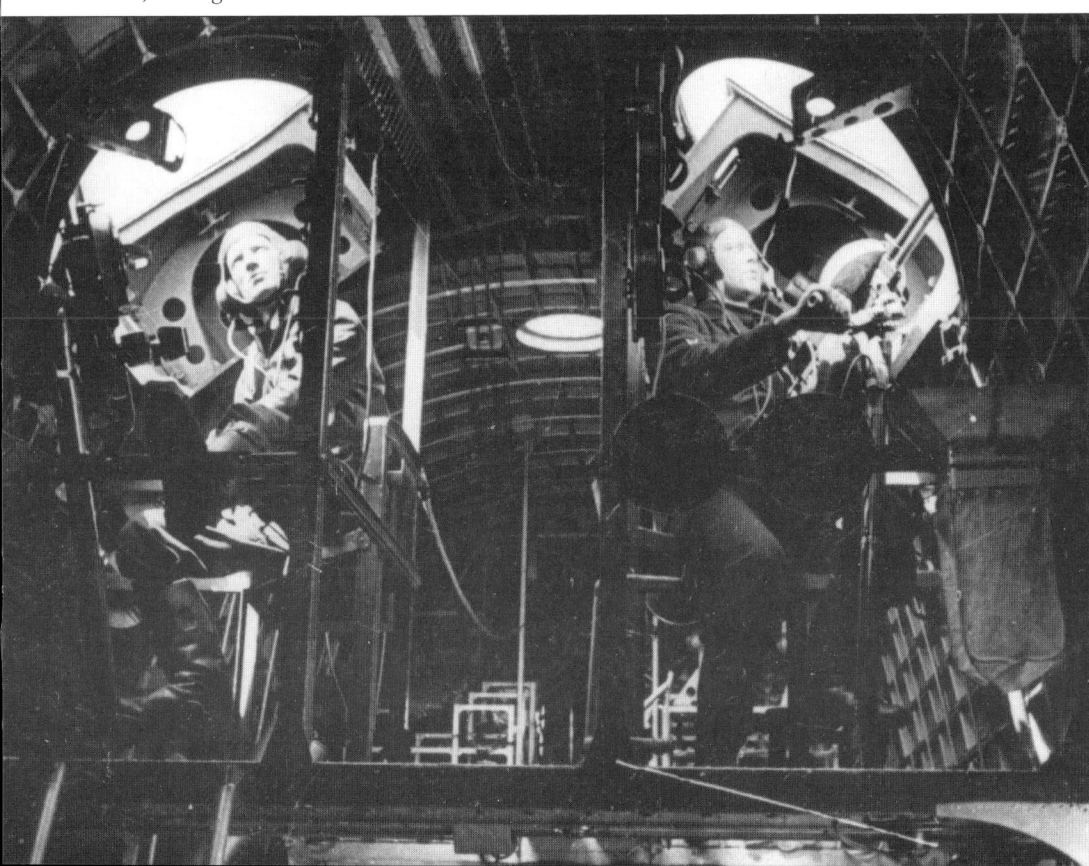

When off duty at night, they bypassed the checks at the main gate and used the dinghy to reach 'neutral' territory, being met by a pickup arranged by a crew member. It had its advantages.

When not on Ops, pilots were required to spend the day in the vicinity of the hangar area or in the pilots' Crew Room. Those engaged on Ops the previous night, or that morning, were excused.

The captain and navigator numbers were reduced when Flight Lieutenant Bell and Sergeant Harris were killed during a clandestine pickup of General de Gaulle's family near Carantec, on the French coast. The aircraft involved was an RAF Walrus. Two other crewmembers were an RAF conscripted ground wireless operator, who had to be given a crash course on the operation of the W/T set and the operation of the Vickers aft gun, plus a British Army captain of the Intelligence Corps.

A clear view of a Sunderland cockpit showing the many controls.

The mid-upper gun positions of a 10 Squadron Sunderland Mk.I, pictured 'Looking forward from rear hatch'.

The side gun positions on a Sunderland.

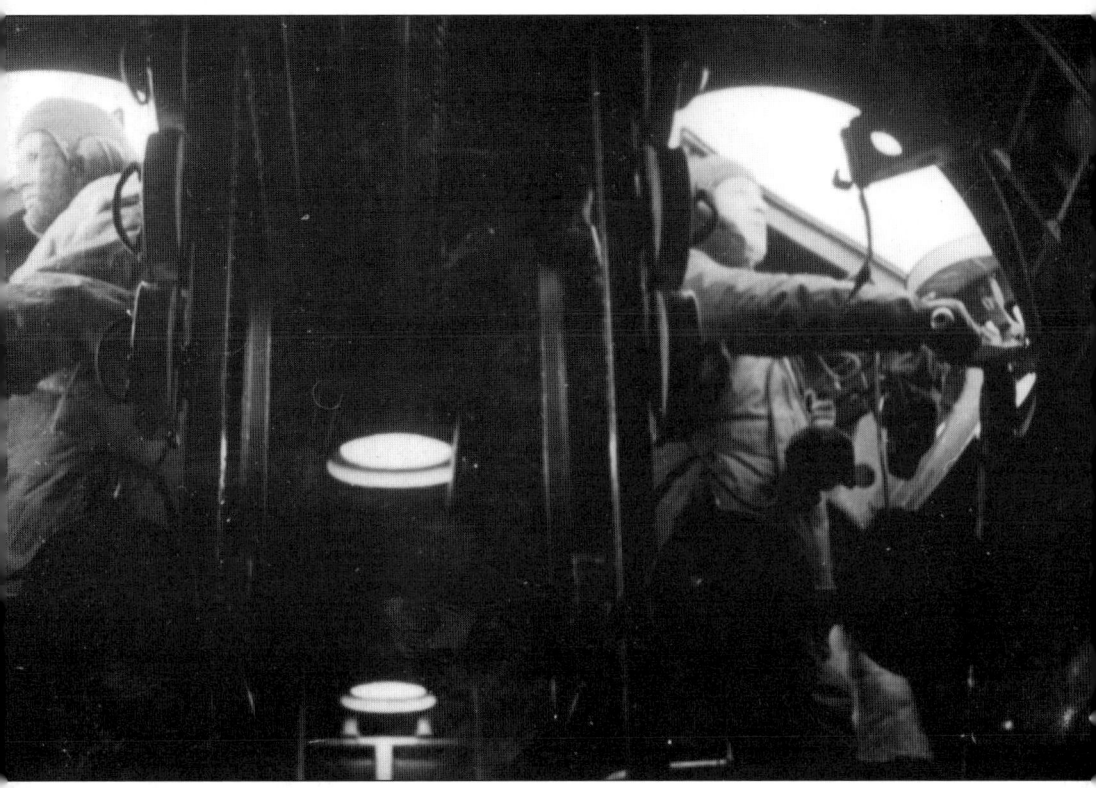

A second view of the side gun positions on a Sunderland.

The authorities were afraid that the de Gaulles may be taken hostage by the Germans and used as a lever to deter de Gaulle. De Gaulle's wife had missed the Royal Navy destroyer originally sent. When it was known that something had happened to the Walrus, a Royal Navy motor torpedo boat was dispatched to Brest, only to find the port occupied by the Germans. Departure from Mount Batten was 03.00 hours on 18 June 1940. In fact, it transpired that Mrs de Gaulle and her children had managed to escape in the last boat to sail from Brest.

It was assumed that due to thick fog the Walrus crew was unable to locate the rendezvous landing point in a short field near Ploudaniel, some twenty miles west of Carantec. The aircraft collided with an embankment at the far end of the field and all on board were killed. It was not until late 1979 that information on this venture was released, and that was only after pressure had been applied on the Records Office. Until then, we had assumed that the flight was to plant a spy in French territory.

Around this hectic time of the fall of France, the squadron was involved in many such ventures on top of the anti-submarine patrols and convoy duties. More about this later.

The starboard gunner on a Sunderland Mk.I. The shorts suggest that this image was taken during an operation in warmer climates.

The inside of the Sunderland looking aft to rear turret.

Inside of a Sunderland's nose section with the front turret retracted for mooring.

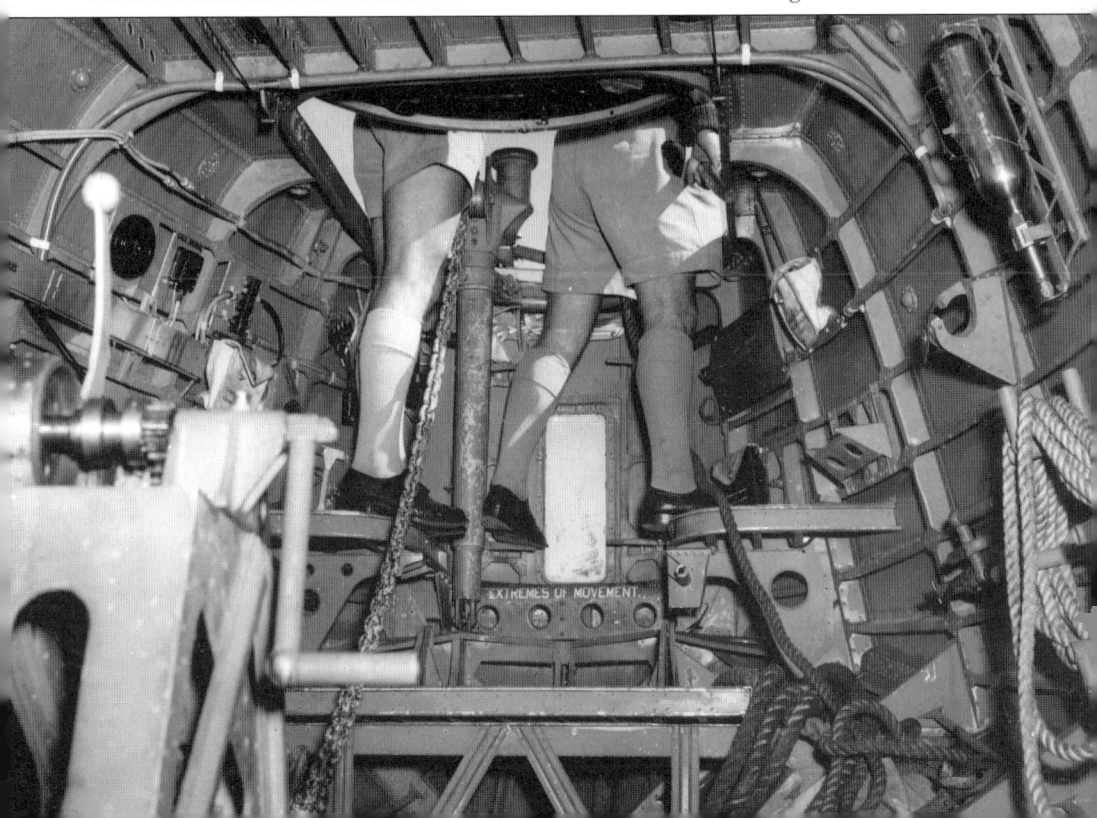

The Engineer's position in a Sunderland.

A 10 Squadron Sunderland pictured flying over Rame Head in south-east Cornwall.

A Sunderland in a hangar at RAF Mount Batten.

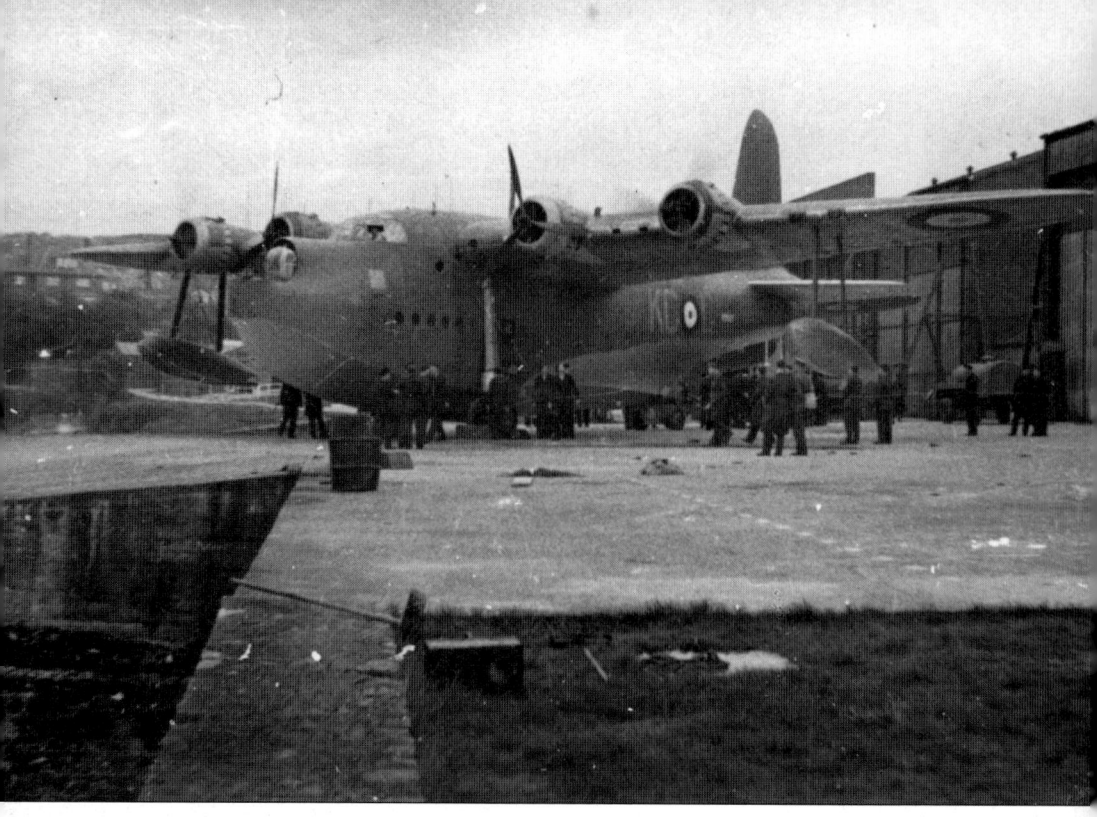

The first in a series of images that illustrate the launching of Sunderland N9021, coded KG-G of 204 Squadron, at RAF Mount Batten.

Sunderland N9021 at the top of the slipway at Mount Batten.

On a trolley, N9021 is manoeuvered down the slipway.

N9021 is pictured at the moment it is about to enter the water.

A view of N9021 under tow at Mount Batten.

Operation complete, N9021 is tied up at her mooring buoy at Mount Batten. Whilst being flown by 201 Squadron, this Sunderland crashed, capsized and sank while landing at Invergordon on 15 December 1940.

A stern view of a Sunderland Mk.I in a recovery ship or floating dock.

Corporal John Herbert Evans, who was serving in 10 Squadron RAAF, is pictured standing on top of Sunderland RB-U at RAF Mount Batten as HMS *Hood* sails by in early 1940. (Australian War Memorial; P04577)

An excellent aerial view of RAF Mount Batten.

My first Op as second pilot was on 13 March 1940. It was a convoy patrol in the Bristol Channel. A recall due to fog at base, PD, reduced this trip to 1.25 hours. The remainder of this month was spent on flying training, except for a convoy exercise in the Irish Sea area.

The squadron moved to RAF Mount Batten, Plymouth, on 1 April 1940. This was a pre-war flying boat station and well established. The location was on a peninsular protruding into Plymouth Sound opposite the Hoe and was bounded by the Sound and the Cattewater, a small inlet. The aircraft moorings were in this area. Later dispersal moorings were laid in other parts of the Sound. Land maintenance was carried out in two large hangars, capable of housing three Sunderlands, and a slipway provided access to the water for the aircraft. Aircraft were launched or retrieved by a winch or a large tractor and the services of numerable airmen.

The new officers' mess, of three storeys and the normal amenities of bar, anti-rooms, billiard and games rooms, etc., was almost complete on our arrival. Apparently, our move was delayed because our senior officers demanded that showers be fitted to the bathrooms before taking over this building. Due to an oversight by the builders, a cement mixer had been isolated in a bedroom, requiring the wall to be removed for its extraction. Another incident during excavation for foundations saw a large number of skeletons being unearthed. After tracing through past records, it was discovered that this site had formerly been a quarantine base.

After three sessions of second pilot flying training, my first trip was a convoy off the Bay of Biscay French coast. The next twenty were also of the same nature except for one anti-submarine Op. The details of those specially noted in my log read: 'MV (Merchant Vessels) 2 DR (Corvette or Destroyer – mostly the former), 3MV – 2DR (French) near French coast. 6MV – 2DR near French coast. 28MV-2DR Nr. French coast. 21MV – 1DR Visibility 1 mile. 40MV – 1DR'

I note that my skipper was asleep downstairs from 02.00 hours to 06.00 hours, and again from 08.00 hours to 10.05 hours. He was the best sleeper in the business. As I was a mere pilot officer and he a squadron leader it was prudent to suffer one's pride. This was common when flying at night with this officer. I am sure I did more than my share of flying with him.

The aircraft were not fitted with an auto pilot, nor any Air-to-Surface Vessel, or ASV, radar at this time. On one later occasion, at night, I was stuck at the controls for six hours, with no opportunity to visit the loo. He appeared, to tear a strip off me for not carrying out his routine when flying the aircraft, to scan the area ahead, with binoculars, then check the compass and instruments and repeat the process.

A 10 Squadron Sunderland on the slipway, possibly at Mount Batten.

In daylight, when not handling the aircraft, one was required to scan the sea with binoculars firmly clamped to the eyeballs. On the odd times when two second pilots were carried, the person 'off duty' was required to stand in the Astro dome and rotate, with a pair of binoculars, continuously. One can imagine the strain on the eyes.

Once I was caught asleep, standing up in the Astro dome going through the motions. After a couple of months of this, I developed an eye twitch and reported sick. I was duly referred to the naval doctor at Devonport. He issued a black concoction resembling thin tar to be dropped into the eyes. The infliction disappeared after a while, mainly because my further flying was with other captains who hadn't the same ideas.

To continue. '50MV – 2DR Returned due adverse weather at base. 22MV – 1dr – 1 submarine-sighted Torpedo! mile ahead of Convoy. No sighting of Sub. Anti-Sub Patrol engine failure 11 hours 25 mins. 20MV-1DR. Convoy Patrol Returned Unserviceable engine. Search for MV 'ANGLESEA ROSE' Found and ordered it to return Falmouth. They refused so we fired warning shots across bows. It complied.'

On 12 June, we proceeded to Brest for night stop and refuelling. This was to give us range to carry out an anti-submarine patrol off Cape Finisterre. We duly arrived at the French flying boat base at Brest in the afternoon and settled in their luxurious mess. Accommodation was in vacated officers' bedrooms smelling highly of perfume. The outstanding feature remembered was the bar. The bar counter was made totally of glass, where a variety of multi-coloured fish sported themselves, and at the back of the bar, plate glass revealed numerous exotic birds. The whole area must have stretched thirty feet. It was a case of early to bed for an early departure, so no opportunity to sample the delights. We returned to base fourteen hours and forty-five minutes later to refuel, having sighted nothing.

Two more convoy patrols followed. The latter containing 20MV – 2DR created some interest when two ships collided in the convoy, and we dropped a depth charge on a disturbance.

On 19 June 1940, during the French retreat, with the same captain (Squadron Leader Bill Garing – just my luck) our detail was to proceed to Lake Biscarrosse,

The 10 Squadron Sunderland on Lake Biscarrosse awaiting return of Lord Lloyd on 19 June 1940.

At Lake Biscarrosse, Ron Gillies (left), Tom 'Lofty' Jensen (centre), and Self, on right, sit on the top of the Sunderland awaiting the return of Lord Lloyd who was negotiating with the French Government in Bordeaux to continue fighting the Germans.

south of Bordeaux, to where the French Government had retreated. We were to transport the Secretary of State for the Colonies, Lord Lloyd, and his secretary to Biscarosse, where he was to contact the French Government at Bordeaux with the object of asking them to continue fighting in North Africa.

Another of our aircraft was detailed to proceed to Calshot, embark the Allied Commander in Chief, Lord Gort, and the Minister of Information, Mr. Duff Cooper, and fly them to Rabat, Morocco, for the same purpose. They received the same response as Lloyd and were extremely fortunate to escape the hostility of the French. The French tried to capture the aircraft, but the crew captured the Chief of Police instead!

Lord Lloyd and his assistant had embarked at Mount Batten that day, and we were about to fire up the engines, when a dinghy came alongside with a case of champagne. Our route was well to the west of Brest, then occupied by the Germans, across the Bay of Biscay then due east to Biscarrosse, to avoid German fighters. We were to maintain radio silence throughout.

Our crew included another captain and my role was to act as second 'Dick' and decode messages on the SYCO coding machine. On Ops these were part of the collection of the Admiralty Code Book (I think that was the name), the card of the period (various letters and numbers printed thereon), a list of the current Verey cartridge colours and letters (for Aldis lamp signalling) of the period(s). The Admiralty book was around nine inches by six inches, green and the covers quarter-inch lead plate – no doubt to ensure it didn't float in the event of it having to be thrown overboard if we were at risk of capture. The contents covered various transmission procedures and codes.

The 'Q' Code, one of the many and used internationally, included two which appealed to us. The first, after the appropriate Q letter, read, 'The natives are hostile'; the other was QRM, for 'I am being interfered with'. In the alphabetic code of the day, it transmitted as 'QUEENIE RODGER MIKE'. Which brings the story to a signal (W/T) received a couple of hours out, from 15 Group HQ.

Assuming the message was important, the skipper gave the W/T operator permission to break radio silence. It was of considerable length and some letters garbled, which required the operator to request repeats. There was no doubt in our minds that the Germans were busy Direction Finding and now knew our position, and, from the message, our mission and VIPs carried.

On my de-cyphering it read something like: 'From the Air Officer Commanding 15 Group [giving his name], To Lord Lloyd, the case of Champagne is to wish you bon voyage and all success etc.' Perhaps the AOC had a better idea of the extent of the German occupation than we did. It was supposed to be a secret mission, all our necks were on the line and we wondered what kind of leadership we were under.

On arrival on moorings at Biscarrosse on 19 June, there was no assistance from the local base. It appeared deserted except for a weird French flying boat (they certainly produced some ugly aircraft before the war) and a solitary Imperial Airways 'C' Class flying boat, that was named *Clare*. Some years later I discovered that the Imperial Airways captain was D.C. Bennett of Pathfinders fame and other ventures. We believed it was waiting for the evacuation of British Embassy staff and departed that evening at dusk, though I have heard that it might also have been waiting to embark the Polish General Sikorski, family and staff.

The immediate problem was to get our passengers to the shore, but there was no one was in sight. A lone purser on the 'C' Class spotted our predicament and rowed over in a small dinghy. Having collected our two VIPs, they all disappeared into the distance. Before he departed Lord Lloyd said, 'You have a right to know why we are going to Bordeaux, since we are all taking the same risk. My job is to try to persuade the French Government to fight on from Africa.' He expected to return the following morning. If he didn't, or the safety of the aircraft and crew were threatened, we were to return to the UK and not to worry about them, as they would somehow find their own way back.

The purser returned to offer us the further use of the dinghy, all we had to do was signal by Aldis. After they had departed, we had sole rights to it.

The next problem was to find someone to organise refuelling. The second captain and myself rowed ashore. There was no one around except a lone boy of around sixteen years, dressed in scruffy overalls carrying what looked like a Napoleonic rifle complete with an enormous bayonet, which together reached two feet above his head and who couldn't understand us. So, we entered the officers' mess, which was crowded with demoralised officers who ignored us. Apparently, they expected the Germans the next day. Not good news for us.

I can't remember how it was organised, but the refuelling barge arrived and promptly knocked a hole in the hull. The remainder of the evening and the next day was spent aboard keeping a look out and being watered and fed by our crew.

Around midnight in the blackness a Sunderland was heard overhead and landed on the lake. There was no flare path. How they found their way to the mooring near us we will never know. The captain and I located them in the darkness with our borrowed dinghy, mainly because they kept their outer engines running. On calling for them to cut their engine – in Australian vernacular – a voice was heard to exclaim, 'Thank Christ. It's the Aussies.'

On coming alongside, they explained they didn't know their exact position or the friendliness of the natives. They had been sent to find out what had happened to us as Group HQ hadn't received any communications from us. On explaining we were maintaining radio silence for obvious reasons, they slipped moorings to disappear into the darkness. What a way to run a war.

The following morning the place was alive with various odd makes of French seaplanes lobbing in and running up on the beach for refuelling. Most were distinctly of Blériot design having a pole sticking out of the cockpit fuselage area to which were connected wires to the mainplanes. They were on their way, no doubt, to southern France. I doubt they had the endurance to get to Africa. Talk about panic stations.

On the far side of the lake there was a very large hangar which was still in the process of construction for the proposed Atlantic flying boat services for Pan American Airways. I guess no one had warned the workers that the Germans were just over the hill.

This congestion entertained us until our VIPs returned in the afternoon. They looked shattered, having had a hard time over the past hours with no rest. The departure was immediate, and we retraced our route back to the UK.

The hangar beside Lake Biscarrosse that was under construction at the time of our visit in June 1940.

Lord Lloyd told us that the French had refused the request to fight on and that there was no hope. Both he and his assistant insisted in cooking lunch for the crew on the way back. They were both great blokes, and I have fond memories of their friendliness and at their 'mucking in' with the crew. We each received a letter of thanks from him at the Foreign Office.

On disembarkation farewells, we reminded him of the case of champagne. He said it was ours, before, on second thoughts, claiming one bottle. The remainder was shared between the crew.

The rest of June and up to 11 July 1940, was spent on convoy and anti-submarine patrols. Before one of these my log shows laying a flare path for an Imperial Airways 'C' Class boat which was carrying Haile Selassie and the Duke of Windsor. Both had spent the evening in the mess. On such occasions the area containing the billiard and ladies' rooms was declared to be 'No Go'.

One convoy patrol was at seventeen degrees west. Normally, fifteen degrees west was the extent of our ramblings, for a reasonable time spent on the job. On

Two of 10 Squadron's Sunderlands in flight.

No.10 Squadron's RB-E, a Mk.I with the serial number P9600, pictured over open water during a patrol.

Another of 10 Squadron's Sunderlands, coded RB-X, during a patrol.

An air-to-air shot of a 10 Squadron Sunderland that clearly shows the type's distinctive shape and size.

another anti-submarine patrol, a torpedoed tanker was sighted, deserted – with its back broken 100 miles west of the Lizard.

During the next trip, on 11 July, another 'CV' or convoy patrol, we saw the torpedoing of a Norwegian ship at 16.20 hours; it sank in fifteen minutes. It was not in the convoy. (This may have been the SS *Janna*, which, having fallen behind Convoy HX 54, was torpedoed by *U-34* to the west of Ireland – she was the only Norwegian ship lost on this date.) A search for the culprit was unsuccessful.

During this patrol I also noted, 'Fired on EIRE MV'. I can't remember why, but this may have been on the orders of the Royal Navy commander to force it back into the ranks of the convoy. Some ships did stray, particularly during the night, which had to be shepherded back into the fold.

Although the speed of convoys seldom exceeded eight knots, some of the older ones still lagged behind, much to the annoyance of the crews of the faster ones. It was always a bone of contention between these 'Salty old Merchant Seamen', who as well considered the Navy as a bunch of amateurs. The fast MVs of above sixteen knots were considered to have a reasonable chance of evading the enemy by constantly altering course and other tactics and proceed on their own safely.

The following day, with our squadron's Commanding Officer, the orders were to carry out a reconnaissance of Bordeaux and St. Nazaire, primarily looking for and photographing 'invasion barges', some 550 and 350 miles from the nearest coast of the UK. As we know today, this would have been some feat had the opposition attempted such an undertaking. 'Ours was not to reason why.'

So, accompanied by the squadron photographer, course was set for Bordeaux – well out to sea of course. Nothing was seen of interest at this place, but photos were taken. At both places we climbed to around 4,000 feet. As our normal operating height was 1,000 feet on patrol over the sea, day and night, we felt a little vulnerable at this altitude. So, altitude was reduced to the norm and an hour or so later (the cruising speed of the Sunderland was 120 knots, or 138 mph) St. Nazaire hove in sight. To start with, once again nothing of interest was found and numerous pictures taken. At which point our midships gunner spotted a fighter taking off.

Panic stations. We turned on to a heading out to sea and a steep dive to increase speed and distance was instigated.

At this time the rigger, who had been preparing lunch and laying the table in the wardroom, appeared on the flight deck very upset. Apparently, two bullets had come up through the bottom of the hull, one of them shattering the sugar bowl. Sugar all over the cabin! He wasn't amused.

When safely out to sea lunch was consumed in turn and we returned to base. Later on, the news was broken that the photography was a loss as all the

A Sunderland about to land on the River Medway at Rochester.

A Sunderland makes a perfect landing.

shots had been of the sky. The camera had been dropped at some stage and the viewfinder attached to the top of the camera was bent.

That evening and night Plymouth suffered its first big air raid. It certainly got a pasting. The Sound absorbed many of the bombs, but a few fell on our base. Not a shot was fired against these raiders that night. Apparently, the officer commanding the anti-aircraft batteries had gone to London for the weekend and had issued an order that no guns were to be fired before his return!

All hell was let loose the following day and the cruiser HMS *Newcastle* was anchored close inshore by our mess, to add to the defences. It was so close one could almost spit upon it. Just after lunch, word got around that their Walrus amphibian was being winched overboard for a flight. As all we pilots had flown this type in the form of the Seagull there was much interest. It was duly dumped in the water to take-off and fly around in the clear skies above. Obviously, the crew were enjoying the sights, including inspecting some of the damage inflicted the night before. However, the air raid sirens began their wailing. The anti-aircraft gun crews on HMS *Newcastle* manned their equipment, pointed them to the skies and began firing at the only aircraft visible. This was, of course, their own Walrus.

It promptly landed alongside to be hoisted aboard trailing fabric from a damaged wing. One can only guess what passed between the pilot and the Gunnery Officer later.

The shattering noise from their anti-aircraft guns during subsequent air raids at close quarters was almost unbearable. It was a relief when the light cruiser departed, especially during any night bombing when we were in bed asleep.

During an air raid on 27 November, two Sunderlands were destroyed; one at moorings, and the other in the hangar, which burnt to the ground.

Chapter 6

Into the Mediterranean

With No.10 Squadron, up until roughly 1943 the basic Sunderland crew included two flight engineers, two radio operators, one armourer, and one rigger, who were all qualified tradesmen and air gunners. They both operated and provided the day-to-day maintenance of the aircraft, as well as the upkeep of their allotted part of the Sunderland.

In this way, the flight engineers – then known as Fitter 2Es – serviced the engines, refuelled the aircraft and so on. The radio operators serviced the radios, and electrical equipment, the armourer serviced and cleaned the guns, especially after each flight as they became coated with salt water during the take-off and landing, while the rigger attended to the airframe problems. They organised their own rosters of watch duty, cooking, etc. during operations. Normally the rigger handled the mooring up and slipping duties.

The drogues – when mooring up – were deployed from the galley hatches by another two crew members with instructions by red, white or green panel lights from the flight deck. The senior flight engineer assumed 'Crew Chief'. As no provision had been made in the pre-war Royal Australian Air Force (we had no requirement then for this complement of crew with the small types of aircraft used at this period) for such a large aircraft, pay, allowances and rank did not exist. So, volunteers were called for from the ranks from LACs to sergeants. The majority of course came from the corporal and lower group. On the appropriate gunnery course completion, all were entitled to the issue of the Air Gunners' brevet. As previously mention, this caused problems. In the RAF, on qualifying for this brevet the recipient was promoted to the rank of sergeant. We found that when our aircrew airmen went on leave, or off the station, they were constantly being arrested by the Military Police 'for the unauthorised wearing of this brevet'. Also, the dark blue of our uniform added to their confusion. Our airmen aircrew also did not draw aircrew pay as such but were granted six pence per day. Big deal.

After each flight, day or night, bad weather or fine, the aircraft had to be made serviceable for further operations. This required, engineer wise, a complete overhaul of the magneto, that the plugs were adjusted and cleaned, filters checked and cleaned, as well as numerous other jobs. The Bristol Pegasus was an obsolete bit of equipment and well past its sell-by-date. For instance, the cylinder valves gave constant trouble by seizing up. No wonder, for they were not lubricated, causing seizure. The position of the seizure determined the amount of damage; for example, a seizure in the open position generally smashed the piston and broke the connecting rod, also damaging the big end and so on. While a seizure in the closed position often caused the loss of that cylinder and the cowling tearing away. All one could do was stop the engine by cutting off the fuel and setting the ignition to 'OFF'. There was no provision for feathering the prop on any of the first three marks of Sunderlands. Revolving airscrews created excessive drag requiring extra power over and above that required with a stationary, feathered airscrew. Only the latter Mark V version, fitted with the excellent Pratt and Whitney American engine, sported this feature. Also, the Pratt and Whitney had an engine life between engine changes of 1,000 hours, compared with 300 hours for the Pegasus. The Pratt and Whitney was used in more Allied aircraft during the war than any other type, including fighters,

Self at the Sunderland controls with a 'cuppa'!

The galley in a Sunderland with (apparently) egg and beans being cooked. (*Courtesy of Andrew Henrie*)

flying boats, and bombers. We were told that fully feathering airscrews were not fitted to the Sunderland as no Sunderland had been lost due to engine failures – these chairborne aviators apparently hadn't read the accident reports.

Continuing with the crew duties, engineers had to make sure the aircraft was refuelled and oiled to mention a few of their tasks. The radio members serviced their equipment which included the ASV Radar. The rigger attended to airframe snags and the armourer, of course, the turrets and guns as mentioned. All of these after what could have been a fifteen-hour flying duty. Should the aircraft require more comprehensive maintenance, the ground crew were called in or the aircraft beached.

Six bunks, a galley fitted with a double Primus stove, containing an oven, a sink, plate racks, food lockers, freshwater urns and two tables in the cabins. Tableware was provided, but mostly replaced by that 'borrowed' from cafés or hotels for the duration, plus tablecloths. These crews were proud of their table layouts.

Backtracking on the crew problems. For about a year from the squadron's formation in late 1939 we were very short of pilots and navigators. Our complement of these was seven skippers, five second pilots and eight navigators. So, with Sunderlands to operate, we were kept exceptionally busy. This was particularly because the CO and flight commander did few Ops. Second pilots also performed flare path duties. Many was the night when one was on one of these and then was the last to take-off for the night on a fifteen-hour operation.

We did acquire a Free French pilot in 1941. Jacques Hazard had escaped the clutches of the Vichy French at Rabat to be posted to Plymouth as pilot for the rather odd French wooden seaplane, a Besson MB.411, from the French submarine *Surcouf* which had been towed to Plymouth after the final evacuation of France. It was ashore in our hangar at Mount Batten at the time this submarine departed for the West Indies where it disappeared. *Surcouf* was subsequently found to have been rammed by an American merchant vessel and was lost with all hands. Jacques was billeted in our Sergeants' mess, and at a loose end, so he was propositioned to fly with us, being short of pilots. Lacking English, he

The Besson MB.411 folding floatplane from the Free French submarine *Surcouf* pictured at RAF Mount Batten with 10 Squadron ground crew.

soon learned basic Australian – swear words first. He had quite a story to tell of his escape from North Africa.

Jacques was under pilot training in France when the Germans occupied France and was evacuated to Rabat with many other French airmen and aircraft. To prevent crews joining de Gaulle's Free French, the aircraft were immobilised by having parts such as props, batteries, tyres, etc., removed; everyone was warned that anyone caught trying to make them serviceable would be shot. Many were.

However, Jacques and a couple of his mates were successful. Apparently, the type they worked on was similar to a Percival Gull. This had a variable-pitch, electrically operated airscrew, and no battery was available. Therefore, they would have to take-off in coarse pitch, which was rather hazardous, especially as the aircraft was to be overloaded.

They departed rather hastily at dawn direct from the park position with a cold engine and coarse pitch. They set off for Gibraltar arriving sometime later. The airfield at Gibraltar in those days was the racecourse situated on the border with Spain. While circling this to determine landing direction, obstacles, and if the natives were friendly, the Spaniards turned their guns on them and shot them down. Luckily, they lobbed in on the British side.

Jacques eventually arrived in the UK to join the Free French. As his father had been killed by the Germans in the 1914–1918 war, he hated them. Jacques became bored with nothing to do, so wangled odd trips in our aircraft, finally becoming a second pilot and captain. As we were short of pilots, he was most welcome, but not too popular with his French bosses. He was determined to settle in Australia after the war, but unfortunately didn't quite make it – though he would have been most welcome.

Jacques was shot down over the Bay of Biscay in June 1942. At the time he and his crew had been looking for the crew of a Whitley which had been ditched by an Arado 196 floatplane. With an engine on fire, his aircraft exploded on landing. There were no survivors. He was 22 years old.

Returning to events in 1941, as an exercise, Group HQ had laid on an escort duty in which a Blenheim was to provide fighter cover for the Plymouth-Scillies sector. We became airborne and circled the Sound for thirty minutes before its late arrival. The weather was gin-clear and to make his presence known he made a quick pass. Immediately, the anti-aircraft guns in the vicinity fired on him. He disappeared into the distance, never to return. No doubt the Plymouth gunners thought the Blenheim was a Junkers Ju 88, which bore some resemblance. Nice to know we had some friends. This exercise was not repeated.

A VIP job was detailed on 25 July 1940, to convey the Duke of Kent from Pembroke Dock to Plymouth. Three Ansons were our 'fighter escort' on the PD-Plymouth sector. We had to throttle back for them to keep up with us.

Our guns outnumbered their total armament, so it all seemed a little pointless. All done I guess to impress the Royal Group Captain. He remained with the squadron until the 27th, when the same procedure was repeated, with the three Ansons, to Calshot.

Prior to the flight to Calshot all the crew were lined up for introduction to His Royal Highness accompanied by the wrath of my squadron leader, Captain Garing, to 'Get into the boat, junior officers first!'

Around this period, of the Western Desert campaign, the odd aircraft was used to carry various cargoes, from VIPs to Beaufighter tyres and ammunition, to Alexandria in Egypt. My first such trip commenced on 29 July 1940. The first stop was Gibraltar where we awaited clearance to proceed to the RAF flying boat base at Kalafrana Bay, Malta.

Delays could be caused by air raids, but mostly by weather. However, on this trip, after a night stop, we proceeded to Malta. All sectors were flown at night to avoid attacks from Axis fighters. We had to fly in the vicinity of Pantelleria, which was considered the most hostile area – Axis fighters were based there,

A Sunderland pictured on fire at Malta following a strafing attack by the Germans. It is believed that this is 'Thursty' Thurstun's aircraft. Legend has it that 'Thursty' borrowed a diving suit and that he tried to salvage the aircraft or parts of it, including a handbell.

plus their form of radar. An altitude of 1,000 feet was maintained but, around this section, height was reduced to 500 feet to avoid radar.

On arrival, refuelling was carried out, a briefing given, and departure followed immediately. Should the aircraft be delayed throughout daylight periods, it was beached and placed in the hangar out of sight. Should the hangar be occupied, then the aircraft was flown to a dispersal point on the east coast, where we tucked it in a bay, close to a cliff, to swing on the anchor until dusk, at which point we would return to Kalafrana for refuelling and night take-off. A few Sunderlands had been destroyed when at anchor at Kalafrana during daylight, hence this procedure.

There were two flying boat bases at Alexandria, one in the man-made harbour to the western side of the city and the other at Abukir on the eastern side of the city. The moorings and take-off area were in this latter bay, which, providing unlimited open areas, was used for night operations. Abukir Bay, of course, was where Nelson fought the Battle of the Nile and remnants of this were to be seen under the clear water and also up the beach, where the old guns were positioned in the sand. The RAF base at Abukir was of enormous proportions. This was the main maintenance and repair unit of the RAF in the region. The only disadvantage to me when billeted there was that the engine testing bays were situated by the officers' sleeping quarters. There appeared to be a dozen of these bays complete with engines roaring away day and night. Sleep was impossible for most of us.

The base at Ras el-Tin consisted of a restricted area in the harbour, the mooring area, a commandeered, rather dirty (oil, debris covered) slipway, and the Operations Rooms plus mess area. These were housed in two commandeered German and Italian yacht clubs. All the small craft were at our disposal. The larger craft had disappeared. No doubt Higher Command had taken these.

The harbour was packed solid with ships of all descriptions – from battleships to merchant vessels. All were moored in lines north to south, which was the prevailing sea breeze (wind of around fifteen mph). The area allotted for flying boats to take-off and land was a corridor between the ships at the eastern end. It was narrow and approximately half-a-mile long. At the time, most of the ships there were from the Crete evacuation.

On our arrival, the load was removed, and we positioned to Abukir for departure the following evening. The return to the UK was a repeat of the outbound trip. On the return our load was VIPs plus members of the armed forces.

Normal Ops followed until 4 September 1940, when we were detailed to search for the prize crew of *Tropic Sea*, a small merchant vessel which had been captured in the Indian Ocean south of Australia by the armed German raider *Orion*. With the prize crew and captured merchant seamen and civilians aboard,

A crew launch coming alongside a Sunderland at Alexandria.

Tropic Sea was challenged by the British submarine HMS *Truant*. The German crew scuttled the ship and took to the lifeboats.

The British merchant captain and his wife were taken on board the submarine and eventually offloaded at Gibraltar. When we arrived on scene, HMS *Truant* had already disappeared leaving three lifeboats full of the survivors. They made sail to escape, though despite the calm conditions, it was a long way to the French coast. To discourage them in their efforts, we fired a few shots across their bow. The sails were promptly hoisted down and we alighted on an 'oily swell'. We taxied close on and the engines stopped. My skipper then directed me to 'go below and capture some Germans'.

I was armed with my .38 revolver and was met by one of the crew armed with a .303 Lee Enfield rifle complete with fixed bayonet. He was an enormous man, and in the confined space of the aft hull the tip of the bayonet seemed to touch one side of the hull and the butt of the rifle the other. It would have been difficult to make full use of it.

Three of 10 Squadron's officers on guard. In the centre is 'Attie' Wearne.

Complete with service revolvers and tin helmets, two members of 10 Squadron pictured on duty at RAF Mount Batten.

On opening our aft hatch these lifeboats were about forty yards away. I called out in my best Australian, 'Any Germans?'

Quite a number raised their hands. I beckoned the smaller lifeboat alongside, which contained twenty men, and these were embarked, and a search made for weapons. All were seated in the cabins under guard of crew members and a 'lumpy' take-off made in the swell.

On arrival at Mount Batten, an escort of RAF personnel marched them off. Later that evening we were informed that they were all Norwegians, and a return trip was laid on the following day with two aircraft – this time with an interpreter. On return to the vicinity there was no sign of the culprits. The wind had sprung up, making a rough sea and no doubt sped them on their way. Due to the state of the sea, it would have been dangerous to land anyway.

Chapter 7
Sunderlands in Scotland

At the beginning of September 1940, it was decided that a detachment of six of No.10 Squadron's Sunderlands would be dispatched to Oban, Scotland, to assist No.210 Squadron, also equipped with Sunderlands, in covering the Northwest approaches. The convoys were now being rerouted north to avoid the threat posed in the south by the occupation of France.

Having arrived on 9 September we set about undertaking the normal routine Ops. An occasional 'dicy' approach up the narrow Firth of Lorne, which was hemmed in by mountains, some 1,400 feet high, to Oban in bad visibility and cloud base down to 100 feet, increased the adrenaline flow, especially at night. When considered by Ops that this sector was unflyable, a diversion was made to Bowmore on the Island of Islay.

On a ferry flight back to Mount Batten we called at PD. The wind was ninety mph plus, and there was a full tide. Owing to this strong westerly and high tide, the water had risen at least ten feet higher. The normal rise and fall at PD was forty feet. The mooring buoys were four feet below the surface, which made it difficult to recover the attachment 'strops'. All propellers on the dozen or so moored Sunderlands were rotating slowly.

Shortly after arrival on shore we were told that our aircraft had broken loose, so I was dispatched to retrieve it. The crew had started the engines by turning on the fuel and engine switches. As the engines were already turning over, they fired up and the crew kept it clear of other aircraft until my arrival. It was a very wet and hazardous journey to the aft hatch and difficult to board due to the pitching of the aircraft. A mooring was located below the surface, and all was back to Square One. Never a dull moment!

On return to Oban a few days later there were severe storms in the Atlantic. As a result, many patrols at this time involved searching for survivors of sunken merchant vessels and ships in distress. One I remember was a search for two reported lifeboats from *Laurentic* and *Petroclus*. Some twenty lifeboats full of survivors were found and reported. Some searches were called off after a few hours due to bad weather at base, while many reported sightings from Group HQ were never located. In any broken sea surface conditions, it was extremely difficult to see small craft and bodies in the sea.

Sunderlands in Scotland 111

Some of 10 Squadron's personnel pictured outside the Park Hotel in Oban. The smiles are due to a few snowballs being launched from the roof of the hotel down onto those below. Note how camouflage paint has been applied to the building.

A moored Sunderland at Oban.

'A miracle' at RAF Oban – two launches at once!

One of a series of images of a crashed 10 Squadron Sunderland Mk.I. This flying boat, coded RB-H and with the serial number P9603, crashed onto seaweed covered rocks at RAF Oban on 24 June 1941. At the time it had been returning from a reconnaissance patrol and, landing in the middle of an air-raid, followed the flare path which had drifted, causing the aircraft to beach itself.

Another view of the badly-damaged P9603 at Oban. Several of the crew were badly injured in the crash; two of the pilots subsequently succumbed to their wounds. An RAF salvage party can be seen at work.

The wreckage of P9603 being examined in situ on the Isle of Kerrera. As is evident in this pictures, the Sunderland was deemed to be beyond repair and written-off.

A close-up of the nose of Sunderland P9603.

Sunderlands in Scotland 115

On 16 October 1940, I was detailed to serve as second pilot with Flying Officer Gilbert 'Thursty' Thurstun to our skipper, Flight Lieutenant Ian Podger, on a night convoy patrol around 500 miles west of Oban. The Sunderland allotted to us was P9600 commonly known as '96 double O', or better known in the squadron as 'Nine Six A Bubble O'.

During a moonlight patrol on 17 October, just before dawn our rear gunner reported a red light flashing in the sea below. We circled this light until dawn, which revealed a ship's lifeboat that appeared to contain a number of people – we eventually ascertained the occupants were twenty-one seamen.

Our skipper was reluctant to attempt a landing on the open sea, but 'Thursty' and I persuaded him to have a go. Although there was little wind, a moderate swell was running. It was a rough 'arrival' on the swell, but we came to a stop after a few bounces and taxied over to the lifeboat. The state of the sea was

This, and the following few images, show the rescue of survivors from the SS *Stangrant*. Part of Convoy HX 77, *Stangrant* was torpedoed by *U-37* to the west of the Outer Hebrides on 13 October 1940.

Some of the *Stangrant* survivors who we rescued. Eight of the thirty-eight strong crew were killed in the attack by *U-37*.

Some of the crew of *Stangrant* photographed while on board the RAF launch. *Stangrant*'s captain, Master Evan Rowlands, can be seen in the peaked cap towards the rear on the right.

such that it was difficult to approach it without damaging the fragile hull of the Sunderland. However, we managed to nose up to it and hold it off while we were pitching about.

Eventually the boat approached the heaving bow, and all settled in. The seamen managed to climb aboard through the bow gunner's hatch. We gave strict orders that nothing was to be brought aboard due to weight problems. However, the captain requested he bring a box aboard, which contained his ship's papers, and that was approved, but nothing else from the crew. Despite their ordeal of two days in this open boat, some suffering from frost bite and the cold, I think this was the most rapid transfer of all times. Four of this crew were lascars and the others British. All were lightly clad, and no doubt pleased to vacate that open boat. Their ship was the *Stangrant*, and they had been torpedoed.

There was the obvious danger of becoming airborne from this disturbed surface. Our other problem was getting aloft with this overload of twenty-one seamen, though we still had to free the aircraft from this menacing lifeboat which seemed determined to punch a hole in our fragile structure. Eventually we managed to manoeuvre it to our port side and by starting our outer engines extricated ourselves from this dangerous situation. Our subsequent take-off in this swell was without incident, despite hitting a few large waves. Podger did an excellent job.

On arrival at Oban, after eleven hours of night and two hours of day flying, we were met at our moorings by the RAF station doctor and our passengers were escorted ashore to hospital. The seamen reported another of their lifeboats, after arriving at Oban, adrift near this rescue position and a destroyer picked them up the following day. All were badly frostbitten having spent over a week in an open boat in freezing weather. Most were lascars with light clothing and no boots. I note that our arrival date was 17 October, my 24th birthday. I can't remember ever thinking of it at the time.

This event was featured in *The London Illustrated News*, together with a photograph of this crew in their lifeboat soon afterwards. I have this cutting together with those taken by the RAF photographer of them embarking at Oban from P9600.

The latter part of November and early December, apart from operations, was taken up with flying training in preparation for command, duly granted on 20 December 1940. I had attained 733 hours on the Sunderland and been involved in seventy-eight operations. Replacements had to be made as the original captains were to be posted back to Australia.

Along with Flight Lieutenant Bruce Courtney, on 7 December 1940 I was detailed as second pilot to do a reconnaissance of ships in distress in the Atlantic

Back at base, the survivors from *Stangrant* are transferred from our Sunderland to the waiting launch to be taken ashore.

Some of the survivors pose for a group photograph at our base.

A newspaper cutting detailing our rescue that I kept in my album.

BEFORE THEIR RESCUE BY A "SUNDERLAND" FLYING-BOAT; TWENTY-ONE SURVIVORS OF A TORPEDOED SHIP AFTER FOUR DAYS IN A LIFEBOAT.
A "Sunderland" flying-boat with an all-Australian crew on this occasion landed on the Atlantic and took on board 21 survivors of a torpedoed ship who were in a lifeboat. "The weather was good," said the "Sunderland's" captain, "and there was only a slight swell. We brought the 21 men on board and took off again very easily, despite the extra load." The appearance of the men is eloquent of their ordeal. (*Keystone*.)

FROM "LONDON ILLUSTRATED"

'Attie' Wearne and Self on the steps of the Esplanade Hotel, which served as our Officers' Mess.

to the west of Oban. For a week or so there had been severe storms in this area, which were still raging, causing the breakup of convoys and no doubt damage to shipping. Our job was to locate as many ships as possible, identify them, give them a rough position and report this to base. The wind was well over sixty knots, the sea extremely rough and the cloud base around 100 feet and lower most of the time. With heavy rain, visibility was very poor in these conditions.

Our operating height varied from 100 feet to fifty feet in order to see anything on the surface. We were so low at times that that there was a risk of collision with ships' masts. Air turbulence and flying on instruments kept us extremely busy. We had no auto pilot at this stage of the war, and I doubt if we had the auto pilot fitted it would not have coped. Anyway, it would not have been prudent to use it at that height and the prevailing conditions.

We did locate two merchant vessels, both of which were having a very rough passage. Neither, though, required any assistance. Communication was of course by Aldis lamp – no radio voice communication in those days.

The cockpit of a 10 Squadron Sunderland taken whilst operating in the UK. The individual with the signal lamp is Ron Gillies, who, many years after the war, flew the Sunderland *Islander* across the Atlantic to Polk City Museum in Florida.

On our return we passed into clear weather around last light by Colonsay, and arriving off Oban we expected a flare path. We circled Oban requesting one by W/T, to be told that it was not laid due to expected bad weather and to proceed to Invergordon. We circled Oban explaining that the bad weather was off Colonsay and wouldn't reach Oban for another hour at least, but were firmly told to divert to Invergordon.

So, I climbed up to a reasonable height over Oban to clear the mountains en route, before setting course, while Bruce went behind the flight deck curtains to sort out the navigation problems with the navigator. It was quite dark by now and we had entered cloud. The temperature had dropped well below freezing.

After a short time in these conditions an extremely loud noise developed like stones being thrown at the side of the aircraft. I later realised that this was caused by ice being shed by the propellers. Shortly afterwards, while this was going on the airspeed indicator dropped from 120 knots to zero, the aircraft stalled and we were on the way down.

Bruce, realising something was wrong, rushed back to the second pilot's seat and together we managed to gain control. We were not sure how much height we had lost as the altimeter had also packed up. We must have been close to the tops of the mountains. With the loss of height and slight increase in temperature, the instruments decided to function and we pressed on. We had no de-icing or anti-icing equipment fitted to the Sunderland in those days.

At an estimated position we decided to descend to Invergordon and the expected flare path – three kerosene flares. These were sighted through our iced-up windscreen a mile or so on our direct course through the heavy snowstorm

One of 10 Squadron's personnel pictured in the astrodome of a Sunderland. It is possible that this was the CO, Knox-Knight.

that was raging. It was impossible to see much through the iced-up windscreen due to the ice build-up, so Bruce had to judge his approach and landed looking through the side window. When on the moorings, it was estimated that the ice build-up was at least two inches thick on the screens and no doubt the same on the airframe. On approach the flare path officer flashed us a red Aldis lamp warning 'Not to land'. We of course ignored it and landed having had enough for the night.

After mooring up and going ashore we were greeted by an irate Group Captain, the Station Commander, demanding to know our reason for ignoring the red signal. Bruce explained our experiences and he cooled down considerably. Our detail had taken four hours and forty-five minutes of day and six hours of night flying.

Looking down on a Sunderland, possibly a Mk.III, in flight.

The following morning ushered in a beautiful clear day and we returned low level down the Caledonian Canal on our way back to base at Oban. This partially made up for the previous hectic night before.

The only other member of this crew I have listed is the navigator, Pilot Officer Sercombe. I can't remember him now, but I suspect he was one of the RAF navigators we inherited at the time to make up for our deficiency of navigators until reinforcements arrived from Australia. I note that I did four trips with him.

Strangely, a short while after this incident another of our 'boats' was diverted to Invergordon at night due to weather at Oban. Flying Officer John 'Red Jack' Costello was the captain. I do not know the full story, but they had been operating all day out in the Atlantic and were diverted due to Oban's weather by the same group captain. They were obviously short of fuel for all of their engines stopped at some point en route – in cloud.

In those circumstances the options were extremely limited. There was only one and that was go down! So, they glided down through the cloud, on this

A rescue operation that ended in failure. This is 'Thursty' Thurstun's Sunderland pictured after losing an engine while landing on the open sea in an attempt to rescue the crew of a ditched Hudson. Both crews were rescued, but the Sunderland was destroyed by the rescuing destroyer.

Another interesting aircraft that I encountered during my service. This is an ex-Norwegian Heinkel He 115 floatplane. It was used to fly agents into Occupied Europe.

dark night, to find they were over a lake (loch) and landed safely; quite a feat of airmanship. As they couldn't taxy, due to 'dead engines', the aircraft was anchored.

The story goes that the crew were so elated at their survival that they were in high spirits and making a lot of noise and occasionally using the German word '*Camarade*'. The local Home Guard, aroused by this strange arrival in their territory, the noise, and the dark blue of their Royal Australian Air Force uniforms arrested them, thinking they had captured some Germans and put them in the local 'Cooler'.

They were not released until our Commanding Officer, Wing Commander Knox-Knight, arrived later. The Sunderland was undamaged and returned to Oban after refuelling.

Chapter 8

Promotion

By December 1940 I had been promoted captain. Further convoy and anti-submarine patrols followed through January to the end of March. On 22 February 1941, I was detailed to Captain Sunderland T9071 with Flight Lieutenant 'Ginty' Lush and Flying Officer Dave Vernon as second pilots and seven crew on a convoy patrol in the location of 60 degrees north, 18 degrees west area. It was a daylight job with an early departure from Oban.

It was customary by this stage of the war to carry two additional 100lbs General Purpose bombs as back-ups, to be used after we had dropped our normal main load of four 450lbs naval depth charges (DCs) fitted with pressure detonator. On reaching the open sea I ordered the four DCs to be wound out. We were at our normal cruise height of 1,000 feet. Shortly after this I heard above the noise of the engines three distinct 'Whoofs', which indicated that we had lost three depth charges. This was confirmed shortly afterwards by my armourer.

The depth charges were carried inside the aircraft during take-off and landing. The drill was to run them out through the hull side bomb doors, attached to the bomb trolleys, two on each side. This was done when over the sea and clear of land, when the armourer connected the electrical connections from these to the aircraft fitting. The bomb doors were then closed.

The DCs were the size of dustbins and not being streamlined created considerable drag, which consumed extra fuel to maintain cruising speed. Later modifications incorporated a lever by the captain, which operated a release catch on the bomb doors from the flight deck, which was under tension by elastic bungee cables. When released the doors dropped down triggering an electrical switch which extended the bomb trolleys by an electric motor. The doors were closed manually. This method reduced the built-in drag, thus reducing consumption less wear and tear on the engines, leaving the bombs inboard until an attack was imminent and also increased our endurance up to fifteen hours (max).

However, the events in February 1941 were a bit before this sophistication. The depth charges were run out and connections made. Before the armourer reported the loss of three, I knew that they had left our happy ship, because when striking the surface from this height they exploded on impact. The noise was heard above the sound of the clattering Pegasus engines and the shock wave shook the aircraft.

This loss, to me, meant that the aircraft was operationally unserviceable as only one DC remained together with two 100lbs bombs. A signal was dispatched indicating a return to Oban and the reason. I was greeted at moorings by the station's Commanding Officer and, in no uncertain terms, ordered to leave immediately for the convoy, which meant no replacement depth charges or fuel. I had expected the stand-by aircraft to be called out. Although I was upset at the time, to my mind he could have transferred us to the standby aircraft; in retrospect I guess he was right, for an operationally unserviceable aircraft covering a convoy is better than none at all, for a U-boat would not be aware of this.

When we arrived in the appointed area the visibility was excellent and estimated, at our height, as over forty miles. It was a very cold day and cloudless

A 10 Squadron Sunderland, coded RB-K and with the serial number P9605, outside a hangar at RAF Mount Batten.

except for one isolated cumulus shedding a snow shower to the north of us. There was an east bound convoy with a Sunderland escort, but no sign of our convoy. Occasionally convoys were out of position due to various causes, mainly because of severe storms, or diversions due to U-boat activity or enemy air attacks. Due to radio silence, any diversions of convoys were never notified.

However, when around twenty miles from this snowstorm we noticed a British destroyer heading at full speed towards it, and then, on the other side and on the same course, a surfaced U-boat belting along at speed. Assessing the situation, it appeared that both knew of the presence of the other, on radar perhaps, but couldn't see each other despite being about five miles apart.

We immediately set course to attack the U-boat, which by then had spotted us, as he commenced diving. By the time we reached the U-boat it was submerged but I could just see it through the clear water below. I felt I couldn't miss.

Then disaster struck. The reduced bomb load 'Hung Up' when I pressed the release button. Though the armourer quickly fixed the fault, by the time we went in for our second attack the submarine had disappeared. We dropped a smoke float marking the point of our attack.

Next, we located the destroyer, now entering the snowstorm, to inform him by Aldis lamp of the situation. The Sunderland from the convoy, who also saw the excitement, was coming over to join the fray. We continued our search for our convoy until the limit of our endurance and returned to Oban. Flight time was eight hours and twenty-five mins by day, and one hours and thirty-five minutes by night. The initial return added just over one-and-a-half hours. Another frustrating day.

Two days later while on a convoy patrol we passed over a trawler entering a snowstorm. There was a blinding flash accompanied by a loud bang. No damage could be found and for years later I swore this trawler had fired on us. However, after experiencing a similar event in subsequent years, I realised that it was a static discharge from the bow gun. During my civil flying I experienced many such phenomenon. They come in many forms.

On 5 March 1941, while out of Oban on a convoy patrol with Flying Officer Dave Vernon as second pilot and seven crew, we sighted a U-boat some way off from this convoy. By the time we had reached his position it had submerged in the murky water. Estimating its position, I dropped our four depth charges, which detonated.

We hung around for a reasonable time and, as there was no sign of activity, returned back to our charges and soon after dusk returned to Oban. As the weather was below limits there, we were diverted to our then alternate Bowmore on Islay, landing one hour and thirty minutes after dark. We returned the following morning to Oban. Our Sunderland was N9049.

Oban at sunset. Note the Sunderlands moored up in the background.

Apparently, the following day an RAF Sunderland was in the same area and sighted a submarine surfaced and stationary, making no attempt to submerge. They didn't investigate assuming it was British.

It was assumed by Ops that this sub was a U-boat and had been damaged by our DCs and unable at that time to submerge. For my 'sins' I was awarded 'half a U-boat' – whatever that is?

More CV patrols followed. I note from my log book that my operations from Oban, dated from 9 September 1940 through to 14 March 1941, represent a period in which I was involved in thirty convoy and search patrols, with a total of 277 hours by day and fifty-one hours night flying. After a couple more patrols we returned to Mount Batten.

The first day of April 1941 saw the squadron return to PD due to the intense bombing of Plymouth and, in particular, Mount Batten. Group HQ had us concentrating off Brest, where the German battleships *Scharnhorst* and *Gneisenau* were holed up and expected to make a breakout. The squadron had a busy time during this period. My log shows:

			Day (Hours-mins)	Night (Hours-mins)
9 April	Crossover Patrol	80 miles West of BREST	9–10	2–45
11 April	Crossover Patrol	80 miles West of BREST. Landed MB	11–10	– – – –
12 April	Crossover Patrol	60 miles West of BREST. Landed PD	7–05	– – – –
13 April	RECO Patrol	Cape Finisterre	9–40	3–15
14 April	Crossover Patrol	80 miles West of BREST.	9–20	6–30
18 April	Crossover Patrol	100 miles West of BREST	3–00	9–15
21 April	Crossover Patrol	100 miles West of BREST	12–00	– – – –
25 April	Crossover Patrol	100 miles West of BREST	7–20	2–50
28 April	Crossover Patrol	100 miles West of BREST – CRASHED (See following account)	9–05	6–00

Chapter 9

Our Ditching on 28 April 1941

On 28 April 1941, I was tasked to undertake a patrol in the Bay of Biscay. The aircraft in question was Sunderland III T9075, coded RB-N. The rest of the crew were Flight Sergeant Tom Egerton (Second Pilot), Flying Officer Tom Joyce (Second Pilot under supervision, on his first trip), Flight Sergeant Bradbury RAF (Navigator, first trip solo), Sergeant Con Gehrig (Flight Engineer), Leading Aircraftman Ralph Bell (Second Flight Engineer), Corporal Cliff Amos (W/T Operator), Corporal Francis Hewitt (W/T Operator), Leading Aircraftman Norman Raine (Rigger/Aircraftsman), John Francis (Armourer), and Corporal Len Corcoran (Air Gunner).

We departed Angle Bay, Milford Haven, at around midday on 28 April 1941 and headed out towards our patrol area, which was approximately 100 miles west of Brest, via the Scillies. These patrols were planned to cover the entry and exit routes of U-boats and enemy shipping to and from German-occupied ports and the Atlantic, and to report on and attack such vessels, day and night. Being so close to enemy territory, opposition from enemy aircraft was expected, especially during daylight.

In late evening, having completed our sortie of numerous crossover patterns, we set course to retrace our tracks to PD, making the customary landfall over the Scillies around midnight and then set course for Angle Bay. We expected to arrive there about fifty minutes later. Our normal operating height was 1,000 feet.

The country was under blackout regulations of course and our objective was the flare path laid in Angle Bay. This consisted of three lighted launches, in a line approximately 100 yards apart. At this point the sky was clear and from overhead one could see the outline of the islands from the waves breaking on the shore.

The main operating area at Angle Bay was some seven miles from the RAF base at Pembroke Dock. There was no radio contact between the crash launches, the base or the aircraft. The only contact was by W/T between the base and the aircraft and that only used for operational messages when on service. So, no contact in the landing base area except by Aldis lamp and Morse code. Red Aldis meant 'Don't land'; Green meant 'Clear to land'. Normal messages were sent with a clear glass fitted. All very primitive, but it worked. There were no

Self, at the rear, 'Attie' and one other on a motor bike at Pembroke Dock.

other visual aids, e.g., searchlight, or recognised radio homing facilities. It was basic 'seat of the pants' flying.

Our squadron had foreseen the dangers and had suggested that a searchlight from one of the local Army searchlight units be made available on dirty nights to mark the operating base's position, to returning aircraft. This, though, was refused on security grounds – a decision that was, for reasons that will become clear, about to be reversed.

On entering the estimated alighting area, I turned slightly onto a more easterly heading to find the flare path. Seeing nothing after a short while, my radio operator suggested we call for a QDM from the Stack Rock radio station situated on the island in Angle Bay. (QDM = course to steer to reach this station). No one in the squadron had heard of this facility before, let alone used it. It was worth a try, as things were becoming desperate.

As the course given was the same as the one being steered, I remained on it thinking we had lobbed short and the next two gave the same course. Our doubts were raised when we estimated that we must have passed this station. Also, we had passed over some semi-circular furnace shaped fires sighted below us in what appeared to be fog or haze. These were certainly not in the Pembroke area.

Suspecting that we had been given reciprocal headings I decided to head due west for fifteen minutes to make sure we were west of the D/F station then call for more QDMs, knowing that whatever was received it would be the correct one, or 180 degrees out, with the easterly course being the correct one.

The next QDM gave a westerly course to steer. So, we had been given reciprocal headings (180 degrees out). Just before we turned, the cloud (fog) cleared and there ahead was a lighted town, which was without doubt in Eire. Eire was neutral during the war and so not blacked out.

By this time, we were seriously short of fuel. So, I gave the crew the option of baling out over Eire or attempting to force-land in the Irish Sea. They opted to stay with the aircraft.

I explained my intentions were to fly due east and when ten miles from the UK coast by radar (ASV) to descend to 500 feet, throw out a flame float, do a 360 degree, turn, come back over this marker, throw out three more at intervals, to make a flare path, another 360 degrees and attempt a landing.

All was set up and I descended to 500 feet on the altimeter and dropped the first marker and commenced the turn to port.

Suddenly, there was a terrific bang. I was thrown forward and remember being dragged under water by something around my head. Probably my head was through the windscreen. I managed to free myself and surfaced. For once, I was wearing a lifejacket.

All was very dark and foggy – we would never have seen the flame floats in this mire. Vaguely through the fog I could see the floating main plane of the aircraft burning on the surface. I splashed my way to this to be hauled aboard by the surviving crew and eventually joined by Len Corcoran, who was the only survivor from the aft end of the aircraft.

Len had surfaced near a deflated dinghy and when he turned on the valve to inflate it, he got the full force of the compressed air in his face. The inner and outer sections had been split. Luckily, he had retained the dinghy and we were able to patch it up it with the repair kit, using my tunic jacket to retain the inner tube in the outer casing. This was a three-man dinghy.

On a head count we numbered Egerton, Bradbury, Gehrig, Corcoran and myself. Corcoran said that when we hit, all of the others were thrown forward and he survived as he was thrown against the aft ladder. On the flight deck, both the radio operator on duty and the third pilot, Joyce, had disappeared. Bradbury had suffered concussion and had a broken leg, but the remainder of us bore only superficial injuries. I think that Cliff Amos was duty radio operator at the time, and he had also disappeared. He floated by after dawn, but was obviously dead.

The hull had broken off forward and aft of the main plane. Three engines had broken off and the main plane was floating, with the trailing edge just awash, the empty fuel tanks maintaining buoyancy.

Owing to the dense fog and darkness the visibility was about twenty feet. A small amount of light was provided by small pockets of burning oil. It was quite cold – being soaked didn't help.

Around first light someone noticed a queer object near the trailing edge above the waterline. It was one of the two pigeons which, carried in basket, were to be released in case of emergency. It was very wet and covered in oil. We recovered the bird and tried to dry it, but we were just as damp. However, we recovered the message slip from the small plastic carrier tube, wrote on it our estimated position (which, as we discovered, was 120 miles out) and the number of survivors and reattached it. But there seemed little hope of our pigeon becoming airborne in its present condition.

We had propped Jack Bradbury up on the mainplane as he was unconscious and the only one wearing an Irvin jacket with a high collar, so we placed the pigeon in there hoping it would warm up and dry out a little. Jack, of course, didn't know it was there. By this stage, we had named the bird 'Shags'.

Around this time, we heard a ship heading for us in the dense fog and it passed close by, but we were unseen. Someone, probably Con Gehrig had grabbed the Verey pistol on evacuation plus two cartridges, so we fired one off. Then, thinking the ship was returning, we fired the other. But it was an illusion, which disappeared into the thick fog. Being of no further use the pistol joined the rest of the aircraft at the bottom of the Irish Sea.

By about 10.00 hours the mainplane showed signs of sinking, so we hung on as long as possible and then settled for the dinghy. It was a tight squeeze. Bradbury, as he was semi-conscious by now, took up all of the floor space. It was only a three-man dinghy and triangular (an old type), and there were five of us in it. The rest of us perched around the edges as best we could with our legs in the water. There was no freeboard and I guess we all hoped our repairs and my jacket plugging the hole would hold.

The sea was fairly calm. Shags had been replaced in the collar – still no complaints from Bradbury. The mainplane sank about half-an-hour afterwards.

Shortly after this, visibility improved and we could just see land around five to ten miles to the east, so we decided to paddle towards it. This was more for something to do than anything else, for we made little headway under the circumstances, if any.

Around this time, Shags suddenly took off flapping madly with wing tips hitting the water, towards the land. Amid loud cheers and encouragement, he flopped into the drink exhausted.

It is amazing that it made that distance considering its wet, oily and cold condition. It floated in the sea like a seagull, looked at us and no doubt thought that our company was preferable to this. We beckoned and called it back. It seemed to recognise its given name by now and flapped its way back to us over the surface, very relieved to be placed back onto its perch in Bradbury's collar.

Around 11.00 hours another coaster hove in sight. But, despite our calls and frantic arm waving, it continued on its way. We had given up hope, when it suddenly turned around to head back. They had apparently seen the wreckage and decided to investigate.

On coming alongside, us we were greeted by half a dozen sailors pointing .303 rifles at us from the deck. Regarding this as most unfriendly, we politely asked them in our best Australian vernacular to restrain themselves. Taking the hint, they threw us a line.

This was grabbed by one of us, but as the ship had some way on, we were pulled under the water and smartly let go. We eventually manoeuvred Bradbury aboard up the ship's ladder, followed smartly by the rest of us, receiving a most royal welcome from the captain and crew. The coaster's name was *Busiris*; she plied the flower and fruit trade between Liverpool and the Scillies. Though a battered old hulk of about 2,000 tons, to us she could have had no greater welcome than if she were the *Queen Mary*.

They searched the sea for survivors amongst the wreckage, but there were none. Not even the crew member who had floated by in a Mae West soon after dawn could be found.

Self and 'Shags' the carrier pigeon after our Irish Sea ditching.

Our Ditching on 28 April 1941   137

The reason for the armed reception was that they had been bombed by a German aircraft a few days before. Launched in 1929, *Busiris* was being operated by the Moss Hutchison Line, a P&O subsidiary, when it was requisitioned for war service on 26 October 1940. While on passage from Maryport to Plymouth, *Busiris* was attacked by a German aircraft off the Runnelstone, Mounts Bay, on 10 April 1941. A 550lb bomb landed on the deck but failed to explode. It was removed by a disposal squad at Falmouth. All of which might explain the crew's initial hostility having thought that they had captured a life raft full of German aviators!

Had we been Germans, they assured us we would have been shot in the dinghy. They had been briefed that all RAF crews wore yellow skull caps when in the sea. I explained that we didn't have time to collect ours. It was the first time I had heard that one and I'm sure we were never issued with them by this time. Once again, our dark blue uniforms didn't help with our identification either.

The first of a series of photographs taken at the Holyhead Sailors Hospital, where I was treated after our ditching in Irish Sea.

138   My Flying Boat War

We were duly stripped of our wet clothing, given a bottle of rum and a warm bunk to thaw out. Bradbury was out for the count and well looked after by the crew. As he was not interested in the grog, we had his share. Shags was taken to the galley for a warm and clean up.

The next thing I remember was going ashore at Holyhead and being greeted by a large gathering of the public. The police took charge of Shags and we returned to our base at Pembroke Dock. Shags, as we found out later, was nursed back to health and taken off Ops. Amongst other bombs dropped on Pembroke Dock during our week in the Holyhead Sailors Hospital, a German mine hit the pigeon loft on the station; the only survivor was Shags.

We were royally treated by the matron and staff of the hospital, including two doctors who saw to our needs. As we improved, entertainment in the evenings came in the form of visiting the local pubs.

Considered fit after a week, we returned by train to our base, except Bradbury with his concussion and broken leg, who remained. Being on posting from the

Bradbury pictured lying in bed while recuperating at the Holyhead Sailors Hospital.

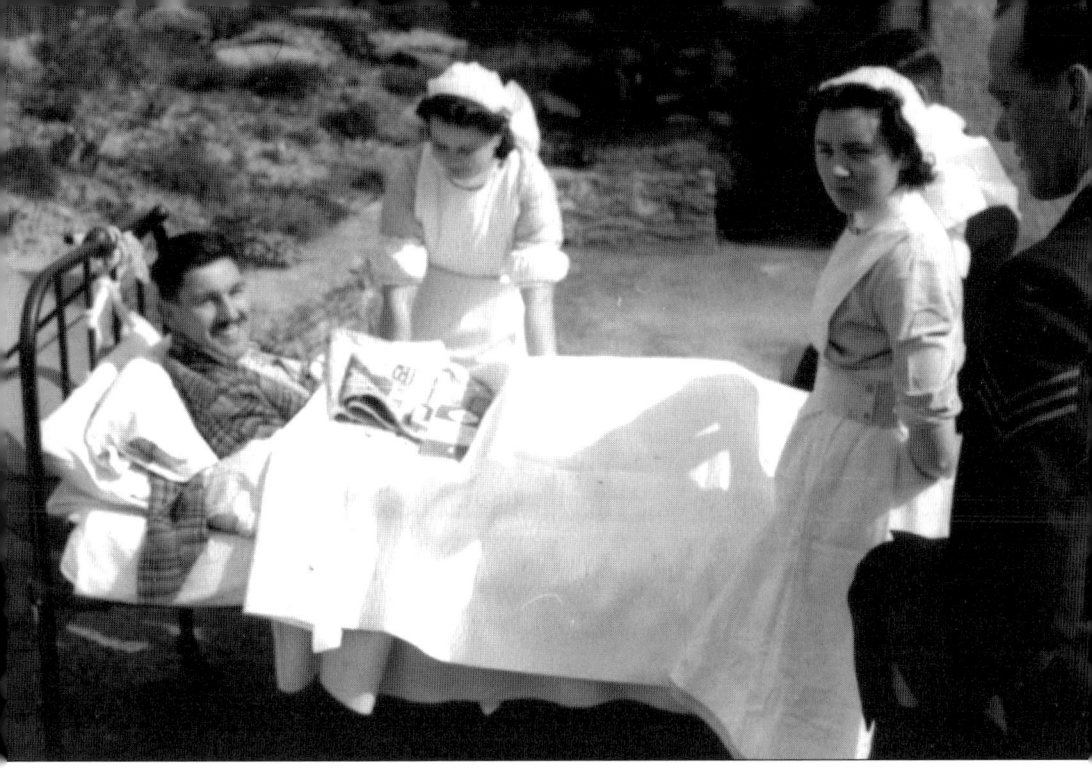

Another picture of Bradbury taken while in bed at the Holyhead Sailors Hospital.

An umbrella provides some shelter for Bradbury while resting outside in his bed.

One of the crew while at the Holyhead Sailors Hospital.

A group photograph taken with some of the nurses at the Holyhead Sailors Hospital.

RAF he never returned to our squadron and the next meeting was at a No.10 Squadron reunion some twenty-five years later at Poole, Dorset.

For me, it was a quick check on the aircraft (Sunderland), a medical and back to Ops – all in a couple of days. My injuries were listed as a broken nose and scratches. Lower spine troubles didn't surface until around 1960. These were treated with epidurals, and the like. Finally, in 2000, I underwent an operation, lower spine decompression/stabilisation/fusion.

The Court of Enquiry, carried out in the week of the crash by an old RAF Group Captain, who had probably not flown an aircraft beyond the old biplanes of pre-war years, when all they had was air speed and altimeter instruments, thought that I had slipped in during my turn from 500 feet. Some sideslip.

As mentioned before, we hit the water immediately the turn was started. Also, the Station Radio Officer was severely reprimanded and posted for not training his radio personnel correctly on the operation of the direction-finding equipment. The basic fault lay with the lack of communications between the Operations Room, at Pembroke Dock, and the Flare Path Officer. As it was, we had no hope under the prevailing fog conditions of locating the flare path or even landing. Our only hope of survival would have been to divert to Mount Batten, had that base been open, for once we were committed to PD on departure from the Scillies, we would have possibly had little fuel to have made Plymouth after passing that point.

The only explanation I can offer on the false altimeter setting which contributed to the crash is as follows.

It was normal during a patrol, in daylight, to descend to approximately fifty feet above sea level, reset the altimeter to that height and read the barometric setting. This was for the meteorological people, giving the approximate position of the reading. The altimeter was then reset to its original position. That is the original base sea level setting. This could be carried out up to ten times each patrol at hourly intervals. If it was not reset to the original setting, then an additional error would be built in on the altimeter to the expected normal daily pressure changes at base during our absence. That is, up to 200 feet.

One could accept these differences in daylight approaches and landings and also at night when in sight of the flare path, but in total darkness, as in my case, there was no reference point in these conditions. So, it was a case of trusting the reading on the 'clock'.

Another built-in hazard was my inexperienced second pilots. The senior one was an experienced pilot on landplanes, but this was one of his initial trips in this flying boat squadron, and the other was on his first supernumerary trip. So altimeter setting errors may have crept in there. I am not blaming them, but it is possible.

It is worth noting that unlike the RAF's landplane bases, of which there were dozens in the UK, our flying boat bases were few and far apart. In daylight one had unlimited alighting areas in an emergency. Our operating and emergency bases in the UK, providing marine craft, flare path facilities, refuelling and maintenance were at Plymouth (Mount Batten) and Pembroke Dock (PD), where the operating areas were at Angle Bay or Milford Haven, stretching from the main base at Pembroke Dock down to Angle Bay. Other bases during the early days were at Oban, Invergordon, Bowmore (Islay), Lough Erne (Northern Ireland), and Sullom Voe. All out of our reach that fateful night.

During daylight if the prevailing wind was east/west or the other way round one could operate either way, thus saving a long, seven-mile taxy to Angle Bay. The latter was used also for all night operations. This gave a minimum run of approximately one mile, but if the flare path was angled appropriately could extend to about two miles. All a bit of a tossup on a dark night and one relied on the expertise of the resident marine craft crews and their local knowledge in this confined space.

Land plane crews, even today, imagine that we had unlimited landing and take-off runs. It was seldom so, and there was invariably a large hill at the approach or end of the run. That and/or a glassy sea or rough surface contributed to the hazards of flying boat operations.

I have a few thoughts regarding the survival, or otherwise, of the members of my crew. In terms of the pilots, although a full harness was provided on the pilots' seats, I never knew of any of us using it. We had a theory that it was better to go through the windscreen than be trapped inside the aircraft and be drowned. Neither my second pilot nor myself were strapped in on this occasion. I think this saved our lives for the bow section broke off (and the aft section aft of the trailing edge).

Of note is the fact that the parachutes were stowed under the starboard bunk in the officers' ward room. They were considered useless to us for we normally flew at 1,000 feet and also there was no point in baling out into the sea well away from land. It was far better to stick with the aircraft and the wreckage, which was more likely to be seen, especially in a rough sea.

In terms of the flight deck crew, at night the blackout curtain, immediately behind the pilots' seats, was drawn to prevent the light from the flight deck restricting our night vision forward. On landing or take-off, the third pilot (if carried) or a crew member sometimes stood behind the skipper's seat to watch.

Joyce was in that position that night – between the curtain and this seat. About six feet behind him was the radio operator's position. This contained the Marconi transmitter and receiver attached to a metal frame. As with both pre-war and wartime items, they were large and heavy. The supporting framework always appeared fragile, no doubt weight saving. It was common knowledge amongst crews that in a crash it was advisable for the skipper to duck on a crash impact to allow this equipment to pass overhead, otherwise one would be decapitated. As Joyce was in this line of fire, I feel he took the full force of this object.

As for the remainder of the flight deck crew, Con Gehrig was seated in the engineer's seat, which faced aft. So, he was probably in the safest seat and suffered little damage or injury.

The navigator, Flight Sergeant Bradbury, was never provided with a seat, as such. He normally used the Astro dome platform, so I am not sure where he was, except that he would have been in the vicinity of the navigation table. He suffered the worst injuries.

The duty radio operator could have been thrown forward as he only had a seat belt, like the engineer, and bashed his head against the radio equipment or table, rendering him unconscious.

As for the crew below, Len Corcoran, the only survivor from that area, said that they were all tidying up the aircraft – stowing loose objects, closing bulkhead doors and so on at the time of impact. When we hit, they were all thrown forward, including himself. The aft ladder, which led to the upper deck and aft gun positions, prevented him from being thrown forward. The aft end of the hull broke off near there and he was thrown out and fortunately surfaced near the dinghy, which he found in the darkness. Much of the aforesaid, though, is mostly speculation on my part.

Of the crew that night, both Con Gehrig, Len Corcoran and Norman Raine had been involved in, and survived, a crash at Oban on the night of 2 September 1940. Len was subsequently involved in a third crash on the night of 19 June 1941, when the Short 'G' Class flying boat *Golden Fleece*, G-AFCJ, suffered double engine failure at night and came down in the Bay of Biscay. He survived, was rescued by a German U-boat and then transferred to a Heinkel floatplane, becoming a PoW for the remainder of the war.

Aside from the five survivors, the following is known of the six men who lost their lives – all of whom have the date of death listed as 29 April 1941. Cliff Amos and John Francis were both buried in Whicham (St. Mary) Churchyard on the Cumberland coast. Norman Raine's body was also recovered from the sea, and he was buried at Pwllheli Borough Cemetery in North Wales. The bodies of Francis Hewitt and Ralph Bell were never found or identified. They are all commemorated on Runnymede Memorial in Surrey. This memorial commemorates by name over 20,000 men and women of the air forces, who were lost in the Second World War during operations from bases in the United Kingdom and North and Western Europe, and who have no known graves.

Shortly after my return to the squadron, I was told by Tom Joyce's room-mate, Flying Officer Martin, that just before Joyce reported for this trip, he said to him, 'I am not coming back from this trip. You can have any of my gear and see that the rest is sent home to my family.'

Martin told Tom not to think that way, but he was quite adamant about his premonition. Martin offered to replace him, but Tom refused to accept his offer. His name is also among those carved on the panels of the Runnymede Memorial.

Chapter 10

In the Operations Room

I returned to local flying and undertook a check flight on 19 May. Then, on 21 May, I was detailed to proceed to Alexandria with Beaufighter tyres and ammunition and duly departed PD to Mount Batten for refuelling and loading. This was a two-aircraft detail, and our CO came along for the ride.

It took us 10.40 hours to reach Gibraltar. We were delayed there owing to bad weather at Malta. Another attempt was made two days later, only to be recalled to Gib. arriving three hours later. The next attempt was four days later and we finally arrived at Malta 10.20 hours later, after 4.30 hours night flying, for reasons mentioned before. It was a case of refuelling and off as soon as possible. We collected a few RAF bods, including a Wing Commander, who insisted on remaining on the flight deck for take-off.

There was no wind, so conditions were glassy calm and the temperature around the 100 degrees F mark. In these conditions, apart from poor performance from the engines and loss of 'lift', it was difficult to leave the surface due to suction on the planing surface of the hull.

Malta had an extremely short flare path consisting of a string of lighted buoys attached together on a line about 100 yards long. These flares were electric and could be switched off immediately if the enemy turned up. The string was extremely short and with a lack of wind they became bunched around the battleship buoy to which they were attached, but with a reasonable wind they streamed downwind, which solved this problem. So, in this case it was a blob of light in the total darkness. It was going to be an extra-long take-off run.

Having reached this gathering of lights we taxied in a southerly direction towards the open sea in the pitch-black conditions. One of the crew was positioned in the bow searching the surface with the Aldis lamp for any obstructions. After numerous checks I decided our position was around a mile from the flares, so prepared for a dash for the lights, which were now very small in the distance. Full throttle was applied, and an effort made to bring the aircraft onto the 'step' so that it could plane on the surface to gain take-off speed.

Despite applying all known methods, it would not rise on the step, and as we could not possibly have become airborne before the lights it was prudent to 'cut' the engines. Also, the engines were overheating.

We retraced our steps, this time to a point where the lights appeared as a pinpoint in the far distance. This time, after what seemed eternity, she came up onto the step to slowly gain speed. I estimated that we would become airborne soon after passing the lights, so pressed on. It was an unwritten law on flying boats that landing lights were not to be used on take-offs and specially landings (as mentioned earlier), but due to these night conditions and not being familiar with these surroundings, I decided to switch them on this occasion.

We became unstuck, Lord only knows what the cylinder temperatures were, in a semi-stalled altitude, hanging on the props – it would have been fatal to have attempted a turn at this time, just after the flare path. At this time the largest mast of a ship I have ever seen (or so it seemed to me) appeared dead ahead, sticking out of the water. It appeared so suddenly in the beam of the landing light and with the aircraft unmanoeuvrable there was no option. It appeared to pass between the port prop and the hull.

Gradually speed increased. I turned to starboard over the not visible low land to set course for Alexandria, the aircraft struggling to reach 1,000 feet.

When things had settled down, the 'trespassing' Wing Commander accused me of dangerous flying and threatened to report me. I explained that no one had briefed me on this obstacle, and that it wasn't my fault if the flare path was extremely short. And, in any case, it was normal procedure due to the shortness of sea flare paths, to stand well back downwind before commencement of the take-off run. He was obviously shaken, but I heard nothing further. No doubt he was, or had been, a landplane pilot of pre-war years when aircraft became airborne after a short run and not used to the primitive conditions we had to contend with.

The landing in Alex harbour was made in the narrow strip between the congested shipping. The aircraft unloaded and, the following night, we taxied out for take-off for Malta and our return.

The usual strong sea breeze prevailed, so one had to maintain a fair speed downwind to maintain control. On a flying boat, when taxying downwind it was necessary to keep the taxying speed a couple of knots above wind speed, otherwise the aircraft would weather cock back into the wind. At the downwind end, throttles were closed to take some way off and the starboard outer opened up to bring the aircraft into wind, then reduced as the aircraft began to turn. The faster one travelled, the greater the turning circle. It was coming around nicely in the confined space when a gust of wind took charge, and the aircraft was blown into the side of a tanker. There was no means of stopping it, the starboard wing tip hit first which brought the bow into contact as well, followed by the sound of crushing metal.

A close-up of the nose and bows of our Sunderland at Alexandria, with some of the damage being covered up.

    The attendant crash boat pulled us off to be towed back to moorings. The bow was stove in and the wing tip damaged. All damage was above the waterline. As no spares for repair existed in that part of the world it was a case of waiting for some to arrive from the UK and that was going to take a long time. One of the hazards of flying boat operation.

    All of the crew were accommodated by No.230 Squadron RAF in the buildings mentioned before, and the next couple of days spent tidying up the aircraft and making it secure. After a couple of days of this the Commanding Officer of this resident Sunderland squadron asked if I would help them out by doing a stint in the Ops Room, to which I agreed. It would be something to do to keep the mind occupied.

    The shift allocated was the late-night period when signals arrived from the desert units for passing on to Cairo. They were a mass of numbers and letters, that is in code, but it passed the night away. Most nights attracted heavy air

Our damaged Sunderland pictured from a launch while at its mooring at Alexandria.

raids on Alexandria, so there was rarely a dull moment. Free nights were spent with the crew visiting the busy bars of Alexandria. The place was alive with troops of most nationalities, including British, South African, Australian and other troops.

Night air raids were continuous. After a week of these duties, the CO asked if I would fly for his squadron as there was a shortage of skippers. The squadron had been heavily engaged during the Greek campaign, then the evacuation of Crete. I can only guess that some of his skippers were on sick leave or whatever. Never did ask. Also, he had a pilot, an Australian, who he wished (hoped) would qualify for command. Would I be prepared to supervise him and give him as many landings and take-offs subject to my discretion. He did warn me that this officer was such an incompetent pilot that he had been made squadron Navigation Officer. These conditions were agreed to and an RAF crew allocated.

I was checked out on 5 June 1941, complete with my allotted second pilot on a convoy patrol, by a No.230 Squadron skipper. Then, on the 10th the CO asked

Looking down in the Sunderland's forward section. It was being refuelled at this moment.

Some of the damage to the Sunderland as pictured from inside the flying boat.

if I would fly with him that night on a mission of which he was unable to inform me until airborne. This request was because his pilots had little night flying experience. A Pilot Officer was also carried to help out. I did notice a sparkling white clinker-built Pram dinghy on the filthy slipway that afternoon but took no further interest until seeing it strapped in the aft end of the Sunderland that evening; by then I knew what it was all about.

Take-off from Abukir was around midnight on a very bright moonlit night. Having settled down the CO briefed us. He had been requested by Admiral Cunningham to proceed to the south coast of Crete, where a large number of Allied troops had been seen by a Maryland bomber the previous day. They were bottled up in this area by the German and Italian forces and hadn't been able to escape during the evacuation a week or so before. The Pilot Officer was briefed that, upon landing, he was to row ashore and contact these troops. Having established exactly how many of them there were, he was to tell them that a destroyer would arrive the following night at midnight for evacuation and to obtain their number.

The CO made a smooth landing to the lee of Galdhouro Island, seven miles off Ierapetra, on the southeast coast of Crete and taxied in to the coast. He then told the Pilot Officer, a South African, to go ashore and do his stuff. His reply was, 'I can't row a boat'. Which meant to me that he didn't want to go. There was obviously no time to argue this point, so the CO turned to me, in the second pilot's seat, and asked if I would be willing, to which I agreed. Having made this 'snap decision', it occurred to me that I had only come for the ride and what was I doing volunteering for this hazardous venture into the unknown?

On my way down to the dinghy the thought also crossed my mind that I may be left behind in this situation, so I shed my clothing except for khaki shorts and a .38 revolver. Owing to the bright moonlit night, I had no intention of staying in the white dinghy if the enemy started shooting. I knew where I would be safest when being shot at – in the water. I stripped to my shorts and retained my .38 Webley revolver, intending to swim for it. Also, I didn't have my identity tag, so could have been shot as a spy. The South African, I had to admit it, had more sense than myself.

The CO stopped the inboard engines while I hurried down below and aft to the dinghy which was strapped against the port side opposite the aft hatch. Everyone was at their stations, so there was no assistance. Once the hatch was opened, the dinghy was unstrapped (on its side) and juggled to the hatch. This was quite difficult with the aircraft rolling in the waves and the weight of the boat didn't ease the problem.

The next task was to tie the painter (rope) to the aircraft and juggle it through the small hatch, on its side, to launch it from the aircraft moving at approximately ten knots accompanied by the slipstream. However, when the dinghy was almost halfway out, we suddenly heard machine-gun fire. Shots then started hitting the hull – seven were later found inside.

We were around fifty yards from the shore at this time. On realising the opposition, the CO opened up the outboard engines, started the inboards and we were on our way. You may understand my predicament at this moment. I was afraid to let the dinghy go as it might knock off the starboard tail plane, and also tear out a section of the hull to which the painter was attached. After much effort the dinghy was retrieved, and the hatch closed. We were well off the water by the time this was buttoned up.

Appearing on the flight deck, not being impressed by events, and the possibility of becoming a 'sitting duck' stranded offshore in a white dinghy on a bright moonlight night, I tapped the CO on the shoulder saying, 'Remember me?' To which came the reply, 'I thought I had left you behind'. I won't record my comments.

However, the next move was to write on scraps of paper: 'How many of you are there? Destroyer arriving midnight to evacuate'. These were tied inside torn up towels etc., complete with spanners, etc to ensure their return to earth, to be dispatched over the local countryside. I can't understand to this day why? Perhaps Admiral Cunningham had suggested this in case we couldn't make contact. Our return was uneventful.

Apparently, this dinghy had been borrowed from Admiral Goldberg's private yacht on condition that it be returned in the same condition and not painted. Being a clandestine affair, the owner of the dinghy may not have known its intended use. He did complain of the paint scratches on the hull; little did he know of the drama surrounding this tiny craft. He was fortunate it hadn't become a German prize or returned full of bullet holes.

Many years later I met an Army officer who was one of the many bottled up in this position. He remembered the Sunderland episode on that night and said that it was the Italians who fired the shots. They became PoWs, had a rough time in their hands, finally finishing up in Germany. Who knows, they may have had an extra one if I had been left behind and survived the shooting and interrogation as I had no means of identification. Might I have been shot as a spy?

Eight 'Middle East One', or ME1, patrols followed. These involved Creeping Line Ahead search patterns. At the eastern end of the Mediterranean, it is only 200 miles across at the widest, so navigation didn't present a problem. So, if in doubt, a heading north or south to the nearest land, an identification of the landfall and then back in business. Returning to base was relatively easy. If one made a landfall where the desert prevailed, one was to the west of Alexandria, but if cultivated (green) then one was over the delta of the Nile with a turn to the west, where Alexandria was at the border of the desert and the cultivated area. There was no blackout at night in Egypt except during air raids. It would have been difficult to enforce. Apart from the Bar 52 owners the locals were not endeared to the British and their Allies, especially King Farouk, who had Italian sympathies.

There were two incidents of note amongst these patrols. The first was on 15 June when we were detailed to locate and shadow a Vichy destroyer. The day was hazy with visibility about two miles and the sea glassy calm. Heading for Beirut, which was then under Vichy and German occupation, the warship was easily found for it was travelling at well over thirty knots and had timed its passage to pass Cyprus during darkness.

Due to the conditions the destroyer's wake stretched back some forty miles, so it was a case of locating this and then flying down it to its source – and there was the culprit. So, the day was spent sending position reports at reasonable intervals with the occasional trip to the Turkish coast to check our position. As mentioned before, it was a case of then flying due south until his wake appeared, then follow it back.

At one stage my 'budding Captain charge' became keen to attack it. My reply was 'No Way'. We were armed with four of those lethal (to us) naval depth charges, which had to be dropped at low level across its bows and that would be difficult enough at the speed he was travelling. Also, it would be doubtful if the aircraft would survive the expected concentration of the opposition's firepower. Also, our job was to 'Shadow and Report'.

As Sunderlands were an important and a rare commodity in that part of the world at the time, the loss or damage of same, while disobeying orders, would incur the wrath of higher command. That is if one survived.

Around dusk, in the vicinity of Cyprus, the Swordfish arrived to torpedo it. Returned to Abukir for a night landing. The 21st saw my second last Op with this squadron.

We were detailed to search for the Vichy hospital ship *Canada*, escort it and order it to proceed to Haifa, Israel, which was occupied by the British and Australian forces. It, too, was heading for Beirut. Apparently on previous trips it had carried German and French reinforcement troops. This of course was forbidden by international law. Also, hospital ships were unarmed and given free passage unless suspected of violating this privilege.

Being a large passenger liner, painted white with conspicuous red crosses on it, it was not difficult to locate. We flew around the ship for some time trying to 'raise' it by Aldis lamp, but no recognition came from their bridge. Our patience ran out after our numerous repetitions, so I told the midships gunner to fire a burst across the bridge next time around. This produced the desired effect. Winding our depth charges out probably gained his interest also. Back came an immediate reply, 'We go Haifa', with a definite alteration of course.

There was no further trouble. The Royal Navy Tribal-class destroyer, which we knew had been dispatched from Alexandria to escort it to Haifa, arrived at dusk. Later the following day information was passed on that a number of German troops had indeed been found aboard.

The Sunderland on which we had flown from the UK, T9071, was 'jinxed'. My two incidents with this aircraft finally led to its demise in No.230 Squadron, which retained it after my departure – the parts didn't arrive before my departure for the UK. It departed Abukir on 21 December 1941, with supplies for Malta.

It was intercepted by two Messerschmitt Bf 110 fighters and shot down. Most of the crew survived and after being washed ashore, the damaged aircraft broke up. Its crew experienced a number of unusual events on the long walk back to the British lines, finally arriving with 156 Italian prisoners – the story of this can be found in *Sunderland at War* by Chas Bowyer.

I departed to the UK on one of No.10 Squadron's Sunderlands on 7 July. After a night take-off from Malta its skipper asked if I would take over as he was tired and was going below for a rest. I obliged.

A while later we were at an altitude of around 500 feet and in the process of sneaking past the Italian island of Pantelleria. We were flying in the tops of some sea fog, and as it was a bright moonless night I was enjoying skimming along in this environment. However, the aircraft suddenly became progressively tail-heavy. I immediately applied forward trim, until it was full forward plus the control column. I suspected some of our passengers had moved into the tail causing this predicament.

Soon the aircraft had become almost uncontrollable in the fore and aft attitude. Thinking the second pilot had fallen asleep, of which he gave a good impression every time I glanced at him, I thumped him calling, 'Get those bloody people out of the tail!'

Out of the corner of my eyes he hadn't moved and I realised he had the control column and was using his full force to pull it back. Things were getting desperate so I screamed at him to let it go. 'What the Hell are you doing?' His frantic reply was, 'We are almost on the water!'

It turned out that having fallen asleep, he woke up with a start and, seeing the aircraft close to the top of this fog, thought I was asleep and mistook the tops for the surface of the sea. He had then endeavoured to pull it up.

What a relief when that was sorted out. My first reaction was that he had 'gone nuts'. The rest of the trip to the UK was uneventful.

Chapter 11

Encounter with a Condor

It was back to the old routine again on anti-submarine patrols 100 miles off Brest, anti-shipping patrols etc. These were all uneventful until 14 August 1941. Our detail that day, in Sunderland Q, W3979, was a ship reconnaissance in the southern area of the Bay of Biscay, off the northwest of Spain. Visibility was excellent with a calm sea.

About mid-day, when we were at a position 100 miles north of Cape Finisterre on the north-western tip of Spain, the tail gunner reported an aircraft to the west heading towards us. Action stations was sounded on the Klaxon.

This aircraft was identified as a Focke-Wulf Fw 200 'Condor'. The military version of the civil 'Kurrier', it was about the same wingspan as the Sunderland, had four engines, was better armed, having two cannon firing forward, one 20mm and the other 15mm. These were more potent than our .303-inch pea shooters. They had a better hitting power and a considerably longer range. This meant to us that it could position out of the range of our guns and fill us full of lead. This aircraft was also much faster by around seventy mph at cruise, which was also a considerable advantage. The German aircraft normally encountered in the Bay of Biscay area were Ju 88s or Arado floatplanes; we naturally tended to avoid them if possible.

By this time, we were flying fifty feet above the surface – the procedure we were then adopting when under attack was to prevent the enemy firing at our vulnerable under surfaces. It also discouraged fighter pilots, who may concentrate on the sighting of their guns and forget the proximity of the water with disastrous results, from pressing an attack. This tactic was changed later in the war, with a suggested height of around a couple of hundred feet recommended. The problem was that in calm sea conditions the enemy could see where his shots were striking the water, which allowed him to ignore his sight to fire more like a garden hose.

The Condor's pilot set himself up out of our range, on our rear to starboard, and let fly. Our navigator had manned the Astro dome position, as normal during air attack, to carry out fire control and give a running commentary. His duty was to take over control of the aircraft, directing and telling the gunners the target, range and when to fire. He would also advise the skipper which way to turn, etc. for, with a stern or beam attack, it was impossible to see the enemy. Anyway, I was fully occupied flying the beast.

We held fire. The enemy's shells were hitting the starboard mainplane; others were making the water by my window 'boil' as they hit the surface. It produced a very uncomfortable feeling.

The navigator suggested I close the throttles and do a flat turn to port, to bring him closer and upset his deflection shooting. On his command this was done.

The Sunderland with its 'built in headwind' seemed to stop in its tracks. The Fw 200 pilot was not prepared for this and found himself in a position about a wing length off our starboard. When within range of our gunners – ours was a Mark I Sunderland which had a four-gun .303 tail turret, two single .303 Vickers GO and a single Vickers .303 in the bow turret. I gave the command, 'Let fly!' At this close range they couldn't miss.

The best part of 2,000 rounds were unleashed from the tail and a couple of drums fired from the starboard midships gun. The Condor broke off to

A Focke-Wulf Fw 200 Condor of I./KG 40. (*Chris Goss Collection*)

The rear turret position on a 10 Squadron Sunderland.

starboard trailing smoke. The navigator gave this information and said I could turn starboard for the view.

The Condor was now heading back to France trailing dense smoke. It was obviously in trouble as it was all over the sky, with its height varying between a couple of hundred feet to sea level. Perhaps their skipper had been hit and efforts were being made to get him out of the seat to gain some control. We followed, but despite his obvious port outer and possibly the inner damaged he was much faster and he disappeared over the horizon still trailing thick smoke. We had spoiled his day, but it certainly made ours.

Not knowing what damage had been inflicted to our starboard wing and its contents, we felt it prudent to return to base; we only had a couple of hours endurance left anyway.

An inspection at base revealed some damage caused by a number of cannon shells, but nothing vital had been hit. Our Ops the following day said that the German base at Bordeaux had called the Condor until midnight, from when another station continued to do so until the early hours, all with no response. So, one can only assume it didn't survive. No claim was made by us.

The remainder of August, September and up to 8 November 1941, continued to be occupied with anti-submarine and ship searches, all interspersed with the odd frustrating sighting of U-boats which had vanished by the time our lumbering 'beasts' reached the submersion area. There were the odd engine failures and diversions due to weather.

To break the monotony, I was detailed on another tyre and munitions detail to Alexandria, departing on 11 November. It was routine this time, but on the return from Malta to Gibraltar we were recalled to Malta due to poor weather at Gib. A night landing was made on our return and at dawn we flew up the

An RAF Saro London, K9686, pictured in Sydney Harbour in 1938. (*Mitchell Library, State Library of New South Wales*)

east coast for dispersal, anchoring close to a cliff in the open sea. Fortunately, it was calm so spent the day there until dusk before returning to Kalafrana to refuel, collect the passengers and make once again for Gibraltar. The engines were misfiring approaching Gib with suspected water in the petrol. Mount Batten was reached the following night and our base PD a day later on the 27th.

The following evening some night 'circuits and bumps' were given to a potential captain and the following day set off to Gibraltar where we were attached to the resident No.202 Squadron which was equipped with the Saro London. They called themselves 'Two F...kall Two Squadron'.

These twin-engine, biplane flying boats were of 1932 vintage and cruised at the 'enormous' speed of ninety mph. They were tough old beasts, but had only an eight-hour range. This was the only aircraft built by Saunders Roe (Saro) that had reached production on a reasonable scale up to then. Like Blackburn, their products never performed to a reasonable standard. This was borne out by the fact that Saro took over the production of the Walrus from Supermarine, so the latter could concentrate on Spitfires, while Blackburn undertook the construction of Sunderlands at Dumbarton, Glasgow. These Sunderlands were of such poor workmanship that our squadron refused to accept them.

From Gibraltar our patrols were mainly Cross Over (X patterns), undertaken fifty miles to the east and west of the Strait, and creeping Line Ahead Overs. To relieve the boredom when on standby at the moorings we 'dynamited' the fish. This was done by emptying the cordite from some cartridges into a bottle, fitting in a couple of wires connected at the lower end by fuse wire and the other ends to a long wire to one of the terminals of a battery. The top was sealed with plasticine (carried to seal leaks in the hull), then lowered amongst the numerous fish in the clear water, then the other terminal connected battery. The explosions were impressive, and generally resulted in numerous fish floating bottoms-up.

Of note was the ever-present oil on the surface in the harbour in Gibraltar. This was the result of all the shipping crammed behind the breakwater. The oil then adhered to the hull along the waterline and was commonly referred to by flying boat crews as the 'Gibraltar Water Line', no matter whether it had been acquired there or actually at another base.

On a forecast of gale or strong wind conditions, when flying boats were at moorings, an Anchor Watch was detailed to board the aircraft in case it broke away. On one such occasion there it did 'blow up rough' with wind up to eighty mph. There were a couple of Londons on the moorings near us and with this wind they were becoming airborne, tied to the buoys. The pilots had a busy couple of hours 'flying' the Londons, trying to keep them on the water, for if they had become airborne they would damage floats or at the worst turn over.

Encounter with a Condor

Apart from our propellers turning and a bit of a rough ride, nothing untoward happened. They certainly kept us entertained for a few hours.

Relating to Londons, the following occurred while based at Mount Batten. Major overhauls on the Londons were carried out at the Saro Works at Cowes on the Isle of Wight. The London didn't quite have the range to fly the sector from Gibraltar to Mount Batten or vice versa. So, the interior of the hull was crammed full of four-gallon tins of petrol which, as required in flight, were pumped into the main wing tanks. This was done by using a Zwicky hand pump.

Due to this overloading, the crew was only allowed to take the barest of personal essentials (razors and the like, no uniforms etc.), so generally arrived wearing tropical uniform, even in mid-winter. The transit of the Bay of Biscay was always made at night due to the Londons' vulnerability – being equipped with three .303-inch machine-guns and their cruise speed of approximately ninety mph. The wearing of tropical uniforms caused friction with overzealous Service policemen, especially when the uniform consisted of shorts and bush jacket in the UK, especially in winter time.

However, one particular crew set off for Mount Batten. They arrived with Plymouth Sound fogged up and in darkness. A forced landing was made in the open sea and they were found later in the day by the crash tender power boat, and were towed to the base. There it was refuelled for the short flight to Cowes. A week or so later on their return flight they lobbed in to Mount Batten for refuelling and loading up of tins of petrol.

After dark they set off for Gibraltar but had an engine failure a couple of hours out, which necessitated a return to the departure station. In the meantime, Mount Batten had 'clamped' with fog again. So, an emergency landing was made in the open sea off Plymouth, at night on one engine. It was around midday before the crash tender located them in the fog to tow them back to Mount Batten.

A new engine was fitted by our squadron and they set off again a couple of days later. Apparently, they missed the 'turning point' into Gibraltar and then ran out of fuel well to the south with another forced landing in the Atlantic. A destroyer eventually located them and towed them into their elusive destination.

Officer accommodation for transit crews in Gibraltar was in the Bristol Hotel, a crummy, dirty place. The rooms were shared with others, the beds of army extraction and a couple of blankets of doubtful cleanliness. All the doors had been removed and the water in the smelly bathrooms was straight from the sea. No fresh water. The food was passable.

On days off, one went to a beach on the eastern side of the Rock. The only access was through a tunnel about a mile long around that was six feet high and the same across. Both sides were stacked to the top, the whole length, with cases of bully beef in cases from around the 1918 era. As the Rock is honeycombed with tunnels, no doubt this was not the only one. Inside there was also a hospital, a large reservoir for water, barracks for the troops, ammunition dumps, etc.

The land airfield in those days was the racecourse situated on the border of Spain. This posed problems with Spain being neutral and, even in those days, Spain laid claim to Gibraltar. As the economy of that area of Spain depended on the Naval Dockyard, when literally thousands would cross the border each day to earn a crust, there was a simmering peace. Security on the British side must have been a nightmare.

There was an 'understanding' that aircraft departing Gibraltar for the UK would bring in as much 'grog' as was feasible. So, to beat the customs, it was stowed in various out-of-sight locations on the aircraft.

The next operation on 23 December 1941, was my last and turned out to be my parting shot.

Chapter 12

Seeking the Enemy

Flying in Sunderland P9605, we had departed at night, more specifically around 02.00 hours, to reach the patrol area off Finisterre and into the Bay of Biscay. Four hours later, at dawn, flying in rain, below the cloud base of 300 feet, we flew directly over a tanker, which was heading west in rough seas. On flying back and circling, we requested his identity by Aldis lamp. They came back with *Berlindra*.

Not knowing its nationality, we proceeded to a point fifty miles away to report its position, course speed and name. This was normal procedure, especially with convoys, so that the German direction stations could not determine their position. The reply was to continue the patrol.

Soon after another signal was received 'Attack'. My reaction was that I wished I hadn't seen the damned thing.

There was a problem for our armament consisted of the usual four 450lbs depth charges. Knowing only too well their habit of exploding on hitting the surface of the sea at height, I decided to drop them from 1,000 feet, hoping at least to spring the tanker's hull plates.

I briefed the crew and told them that after release of our charges, I would dive for the water to get out of range of their guns, flatten out, and then, once at a safe distance, climb back to a position to photograph and observe. The navigator went below to set up the bomb aimer's position, taking a newly introduced hand-held bombsight. So, we were committed.

Normally in low-level attacks on submarines the depth charges were released on the captain's judgement. There were no 'implements' fitted for this and the captain was too occupied to have his attention diverted from his main job.

On arrival back at the tanker we found that it had turned about and was now heading east. Either it had been recalled by its control or, having been detected by us and therefore certain to receive due attention from the Royal Navy and RAF, its captain had made the decision to turn for home. Being fully laden it was either a supply vessel for U-boats or armed merchant raiders. On previous voyages it had supplied armed merchant raiders in the southern Indian Ocean.

The cloud had lifted to around 1,000 feet by the time of our next contact and the tanker was making heavy weather in the turbulent seas. We were plugging into a strong wind and my effort to straddle him was met by him turning to port

A picture we took from our Sunderland of the German tanker *Berlindra* which was attacked on 23 December 1941.

as we approached on his starboard side. After what seemed like an eternity, we finally passed over his bows to be greeted with anti-aircraft fire. The navigator gave 'Bombs away', at which point we dived for the safety of the lower level. At this moment a couple of bumps shook the aircraft.

On levelling out the navigator appeared on the flight deck looking distressed and very white. On asking why he said, 'Christ, I thought we'd had it and were about to crash'. Apparently, he hadn't heard my briefing on diving after the bombs had been released. He also added, 'You ought to have a look below'.

Our return to the tanker revealed it listing to port and, trailing a considerable amount of oil, steaming at a reduced speed estimated at four knots. It had previously been making around ten knots. Photos were taken, speed and course noted and a signal sent to base on the results.

After this, I went below to check the navigator's remark to find two holes of about two feet in diameter, one in the wardroom directly under the flight deck, the other just aft of the hull step. Both were dead centre, hitting the keel member, which is probably the strongest part of the hull. If they hadn't hit and exploded there, they would have most likely exploded inside, causing havoc. Some shrapnel had penetrated the flight deck, which was not found until later. It was fortunate that the German gunner was such a good shot. Also, our only casualty was the second fitter (flight engineer in modern parlance) who sustained shrapnel wounds in his right arm.

Not knowing what further damage had been inflicted in the main planes, it was prudent to return to base. Also, a day landing had to be made for there was the added problem of maintaining the aircraft afloat long enough to allow beaching. The night landing area at Angle Bay was six miles from the base and slipway. With these holes in the hull, it wouldn't have remained afloat that long. So, it was a case of landing close to the warping buoy off the slipway and immediately being hauled ashore.

When the depth charges had exploded, the navigator said that the tall columns of water obscured the ship's bridge and the tail gunner reported a large volume of smoke, followed by the vessel trailing an oil streak 200 yards wide.

When making a landfall at the Isles of Scilly, a Ju 88 flew around us but did not get within range. We were pleased to see him move off for we had had enough excitement for one day.

In our signal to base we gave estimated damage to ourselves, including 'BEACH ONE'. We had a code to indicate priority of damage and urgency of beaching. The code 'BEACH ONE' indicated that we required immediate beaching. 'BEACH TWO' would have instructed those ashore that we needed beaching, but that it did not need to be immediately, whilst 'BEACH THREE' indicated that we only required beaching for investigation.

It was obvious on arrival overhead, from the number of marine craft in the area and spectators ashore, that our message had had the desired effect. I lobbed the aircraft down by the warping buoy and we made fast. All Hell was then let loose.

Beaching gear was hastily attached, with the boats getting in each other's way, while we aboard were busy bailing out the damaged bilges. As was normal, before landing (and as well as take-off) the cabin's watertight doors had been clamped into position. In addition, some of the bunk mattresses had been bunged into the two gaping holes. These were then stood on by crew members during and after landing to reduce the inflow of water. Things were getting desperate by the time the Sunderland was beached.

An hour-and-a-half after my attack, another of our squadron's aircraft sighted the tanker, which was listing to starboard and still trailing a wide oil slick. His radio had broken down and was returning to base. He didn't attack, for without W/T communications, he was unable to establish whether it was British or alien and had no authority to attack. The ship was photographed but was not fired upon.

These photos enabled this tanker to be identified as *Ole Jacob* (8,306 tons), a former Norwegian vessel now in German hands and renamed MV *Benno*. *Ole Jacob* was captured in the Indian Ocean by the German raider *Atlantis* on

11 October 1940. She had previously been used to supply the German raider *Orion*, prior to her return to Bordeaux on 19 July 1941.

The following day another of our Sunderlands was dispatched to intercept the tanker before it could reach a French port. On arrival, they discovered that the tanker was being escorted by Ju 88 fighters. The skipper positioned for an attack on the ship and while dropping his depth charges experienced heavy anti-aircraft opposition from the vessel. These depth charges fell thirty yards ahead. He was also attacked by the fighters.

Meanwhile, the destroyer HMS *Vanoc* was near the scene and was also attacked by the Ju 88s, causing an explosion onboard. The skipper drove off the offending aircraft but was forced to return to base (Gibraltar?) due to heavy fuel consumption and damage.

Later a Bristol Beaufort from an RAF squadron carried out a torpedo attack. The ship was beached at Puerto Carino on the northwest coast of Spain. Apparently, the Spanish were not pleased having an attack made in their territorial waters and protested. They were pro-German, so I guess it was considered 'fair game' by the British.

Having spent two years on operations, totalling 173 sorties in 1,800 hours flying, I was informed that I was to be posted back to Australia. For the first week of my last days in the squadron, in January 1942 I was detailed to survey Poole Harbour as a likely RAF operating base.

British Overseas Airways Corporation (BOAC) had been based there with its flying boats since 1 April 1940. My report suggested it as unsuitable due to shortness of take-off areas, plus obstacles in the water and on the shore (anti-landing defences, etc). BOAC normally flew from there in daylight and these hazards would present problems during night flying. This report was ignored, and an RAF base set up with a newly formed No.461 Squadron RAAF taking residence in 1942. It was not a success, and this squadron was moved to Pembroke Dock where it stayed for the duration. Another RAF squadron replaced it, but was also removed a short while after occupation.

Before I leave my account of my time on No.10 Squadron, I should mention that the order detailing crews and aircraft for the following day appeared on the Crew Notice Board. The officer pilots and navigator were transported from the mess to operations, and there briefed. Should the navigator or a pilot be a sergeant, they were not permitted in the Operations Room. This was unfair, especially for the navigator as he wouldn't have a clue as to where he was going until a couple of minutes before departure.

At night the Duty Station Sergeant was responsible for calling the officers and collecting the two pigeons, which were confined in a small wicker basket. They remained there throughout the trip – sometimes ten hours or more in the darkness. The crew fed and watered them. Normally, when we returned at a reasonable hour in daylight and passed the Scillies or equivalent landfall, they would be thrown out to fly home. In order to prevent damage to their feathers when launched into the 120-knot slipstream they were wrapped in newspaper with the idea that the paper would fall away to free them for flight. I often wondered how many reached their lofts. Perhaps this accounts for the accumulations of pigeons seen today which have turned wild. No doubt their forebears considered that enduring such a departure once, was one too many and didn't return.

Before launching, I think, the message form contained in the small carrier attached to its leg was removed. If it was found intact on return, then it was assumed the aircraft was in difficulties and the appropriate action taken. In these circumstances, if one had time then this form would be filled in and placed in the container.

After my time with the squadron, the poor reliability of the Pegasus engines deteriorated further. It was unusual for one to reach 300 hours before having to be changed. When one considers the life of modern jet engines is 22,000 hours, with some 'on the wing' (not removed) for three years, it gives some idea how things have improved. The armament also was considered insufficient to counteract the opposition experienced.

As the aircraft belonged to Australia, a move was made to rectify these deficiencies. It came to a head when a new Sunderland replacement required seven engine changes before it became operational. Many of the engines fitted at this time were overhauled ex-Wellington ones, which, with poor workmanship at 'shadow' factories, failed to reach a reasonable standard.

So, it was decided, later in the war, to modify a Sunderland and fit American Pratt and Whitney Twin Wasp R1830 engines of 1,200hp, complete with fully feathering airscrews. This, apart from the extra 150hp, was a sophisticated piece of equipment for the time, very reliable with a life of 1,000 hours between engine changes. It was used in most American military aircraft and reputed to be the most produced engine of the war.

The squadron contacted Group HQ and Short Brothers on their proposed conversion but received little enthusiasm from both. Their opinion was that, due to the extra weight and power, the main spar would not be strong enough to support the Pratt and Whitney units. However, under pressure, it was later admitted that Short Brothers had carried out further tests which proved it would be satisfactory.

So, four Pratt and Whitney engines were scrounged. The official said, 'Yes, but' they didn't have the spare capacity at factories to facilitate this modification. The squadron said they would carry out the mod, provided a spare aircraft was made available. This was reluctantly agreed to and work commenced in December 1943 at Mount Batten, using squadron personnel and the advice of a Short Brothers' test pilot and a couple of metal workers from Blackburn (who built this particular aircraft).

The squadron's modification was based on the Catalina installation. The aircraft was flown successfully in April 1944. At the same time Short Brothers modified another Sunderland at Rochester along the same lines. The main differences were the petrol line routing, engine starting panel and, also, on their system, the fact that the engine would shut down if the control line hydraulic was shot away.

No.10 Squadron's ideas were adopted in these cases and the modification considered a remarkable improvement. A number of Mark IIIs were converted,

A Sunderland's interior showing the lateral gun positions. Note the belt-fed .5-inch machine-guns in the ports on each side.

but it was late in the war and so had little opportunity to prove its value. Today only seven out of the 749 Sunderlands built remain and they are all Mark V versions. The examples that are located at Hendon, Duxford and MOTAT, Auckland in New Zealand, are Sunderlands, while two civil conversions to Sandringhams can be seen at Le Bourget, Paris, and in Southampton's Solent Sky Museum.

Strangely No.10 Squadron never operated the Mark V. Probably because of the extra costs involved and also it was near the end of the war in Europe.

The Pegasus was rated at 1,050hp and didn't have a feathering airscrew. The valves could run dry, which caused them to seize. Sometimes this was with disastrous results, such as valves dropping into the cylinders, or seizing causing the cylinder to blow off, taking the cowling with it and sometimes cause engine fires. The Pratt and Whitney, in addition, had fuel flow meters and feathering airscrews. Unfortunately, the bomb load was increased and additional equipment installed which raised the All Up Weight from 58,000lbs to 60,000lbs. So, take-off performance stayed almost the same, but the Pratt and Whitney engine made up for it all.

There were two further modifications. These were the fitting of four fixed .303-inch Browning machine-guns to the bow, operated by the skipper, and a B 17 type cut-out on either side of the 'midship' position with installation of a 0.5-inch gun each side. These were a considerable improvement to the .303 weapons fitted at other positions, but had a restricted arc of fire.

About September 1943, Grand Admiral Dönitz ordered all U-boats to remain on surface to fight it out with naval and Allied aircraft. Later in the war, the U-boats were fitted with an enclosed platform aft of the conning tower, armed with a four-gun 20mm unit and two double gun 20mm units. Quite a concentration of firepower.

As these U-boats operated in pairs, they presented a formidable target to attacking aircraft. Their cannon outranged the opposition's .303-inch 'pea shooters' and a number of aircraft were shot down. The .303s may have contributed to the skipper's morale, but not to the second pilot observing the action. The only armour plate fitted to the Sunderland was a panel attached to the back of the skipper's seat, which was no protection when attacked from the front.

To resume. My next posting was to RAAF Overseas HQ, Kodak House, London, to await transport to Australia. On 12 January 1942, I was married and the remainder of the time before my departure was spent visiting various places of interest, such as the aircraft test centre Boscombe Down and Short Brothers at Rochester.

Before marriage, it was customary to obtain the permission of the Commanding Officer for Flight Lieutenants and below (my rank was the former). This was done to my ex-CO who then was in charge of the Personnel Department at that time. He blew his top, saying I had been selected to fly a Sunderland to Australia carrying the RAAF Air Officer Commanding this unit, Air Marshal 'Dickie' Williams, and also to be his personal assistant. So, I was wheeled into his office to be introduced and the news broken to him of my intentions. I feel my ex-CO expected him to rebuke me, but he came from behind his desk and shook me by the hand to congratulate me.

Both my ex-CO and myself were taken aback and I for one was pleased, but my ex-CO was a bit deflated. Anyhow, it never came off, possibly because the Japanese were active near Singapore (this island fortress fell on 15 February 1942) and there were no Sunderland spares east of Alexandria. It seemed a bit ambitious and unworkable anyhow.

On 27 April 1942 we embarked on the MV *Glenorchy* of 10,000 tons, which sailed from Liverpool. It was a merchant ship, which normally carried some ten passengers. The cabin accommodation was doubled up so we mustered a total of twenty passengers. They were all services personnel apart from a few civilians in government jobs, plus wives. The couple who shared the cabin opposite us had just been married like ourselves. He was a New Zealander and an air gunner who had completed his tour in Bomber Command.

Glenorchy was loaded to the 'gunnels' with a variety of arms ranging from tanks to bicycles. On deck were five Bristol Beaufighters, three on the forward deck and two aft. These disappeared into the Atlantic in the early stages due to high seas breaking over the ship. The cargo was destined for Australia and New Zealand.

Married English Girl

Strains of "Waltzing Matilda," played by Carol Gibbons, attracted the attention of dancers at the Savoy, London, when Flight-Lieut. Victor Hodgkinson, R.A.A.F., formerly of Sydney, and his fair-haired Essex bride, Theresa Myers, danced there with members of their wedding party.

In a few minutes celebrities were toasting the bride and bridegroom.

Flight-Lieutenant Hodgkinson is one of the most popular members of No. 10 Squadron. Nicknamed "Plunker," he is also one of the squadron's aces.

Flight-Lieutenant A. G. H. Wearn, of Perth, was best man. Guests included Squadron-Leader Ron Cross, A.F.C., instructor from Point Cook and Narromine, who recently arrived in England to join a night fighter squadron. Flight-Lieutenant Hodgkinson was one of his pupils.

Also present were Squadron-Leader Hugh Birch, D.F.C., Flight-Lieutenants J. B. King, Reg Marks, Gil Thurston, Buck Judell, and John Costello, who was accompanied by his wife.

Flying-Officers Douglas White and Bill Tavenner were also present.

The wedding took place at Romford, Essex.

Vic and Terry's marriage announcement in an Australian newspaper.

Seeking the Enemy 169

Vic and Terry on their wedding day.

Vic and Terry during their passage to Australia in 1942.

The day after departure, my New Zealand friend and I offered the captain our services as lookouts. This was duly accepted. We worked daylight shifts and helped to fill in the time. The weather was poor during our transit of the Atlantic and it didn't really clear until well south. Our track took a line due west to the centre of the Atlantic, then due south to a point due east of Colon, Panama, and direct to that port.

As the ship cruised at sixteen knots there was no escort provided. It was armed with a four-inch naval gun and a four-inch (approximately) anti-aircraft gun that was manned by Army personnel. There were also two Bofors, one fore and one aft. There were a couple of old Hotchkiss .300 calibre, web-belt-fed machine-guns on the bridge.

The ship had been built at Hong Kong in 1940, so was reasonably new and very comfortable. Fresh water was on tap all the time. Blue Funnel Line were its owners, and the crew, apart from the British officers, were Chinese.

Two British aircraft were sighted a few days out and there wasn't any further excitement until a few days out from Colon. We were ploughing along in a calm sea and cloudless sky when I sighted what turned out to be a Belfast-type heavy cruiser heading for us.

Its signal lamp was flashing, 'What ship?' Our skipper, who had been notified of the sighting, showed little interest and seemed to ignore both my message and the signal which was being flashed continuously. The situation was resolved when the cruiser signalled, 'Stop'. This was ignored, at which point the next thing I heard was a loud explosion from this ship followed by a large splash close to the bow of our ship.

This concentrated our Captain's mind and he ordered full reverse, causing *Glenorchy* to come to a 'Dead halt'. The cruiser then proceeded to circle us from a distance with all of its guns pointed menacingly at us. Our skipper had by then called the wireless operator onto the bridge to deal with the flow of messages passed between the two ships. Having now been satisfied with our identity, the cruiser shot off into the distance at a rate of knots. Apparently, a sister ship of our type had been captured off Norway early in the war and had been converted to an armed raider. So naturally the Navy was more than cautious when approaching us.

A few days were spent at Colon refuelling and the like, before we passed through the Panama Canal. From Panama we proceeded due west for some days to set course to the south, running from the stable tropical waters to the turbulent South Pacific, where course was set to round the southern tip of New Zealand and up to Wellington. In retrospect our track must have been around the 48th parallel. This area is generally referred to as the 'Roaring Forties and the Screaming Fifties'. To this I will readily agree. For days on end the ship plunged into enormous seas and at times was stationary (albeit with enough way on to maintain control), when the ship would be completely engulfed by giant waves. It was a very uncomfortable for a couple of weeks and all were pleased when course was set to the north. This route was taken to avoid submarines and the armed raiders known to be operating in these areas.

On arrival at Wellington some of the tanks, armament and so on were offloaded, which took a number of days. The ship had been loaded with the ammunition stowed at the bottom, the tanks next and the lighter cargo on top. As the skipper said, it was loaded that way in case of the ammunition exploding, then the tanks etc, would absorb some of the blast.

The break at Wellington enabled us to see some of the sights of the North Island. A couple of days were spent at Sydney before proceeding to Melbourne to report to RAAF Headquarters. A week's leave was granted. I was also posted to No.3 Operational Training Unit (OTU) at Rathmines for conversion to the Consolidated Catalina flying boat.

Chapter 13

The Flying Cats

At this stage my rank was Flight Lieutenant, having been promoted on 1 August 1941. RAAF Station Rathmines was situated eighty miles to the north of Sydney and twenty miles to the south of Newcastle, on one of the beautiful lakes which stretch along this picturesque coast. It was a lovely situation and referred to as the 'best club in the RAAF'. The Operational

An aerial view of RAAF Rathmines. Note the numerous Catalinas on the water. (*Courtesy of Penny Fearner*)

An air-to-air shot of Catalina A24-10 – my aircraft.

Another Catalina at Rathmines, this time photographed on its beaching gear.

Training Unit catered for both Catalina and Seagull (Walrus) training. Also based on the station was the Flying Boat Maintenance Unit and No.9 Squadron, the latter flew the Vought Sikorsky OS2U Kingfisher float planes, whose job was to patrol the sea off the local coast and escort convoys.

My Catalina course commenced on 13 May 1942. This course included the normal exercises of take-off and landing, day and night, in varying conditions, stalls, stall landings, cruise control handling, feathering, taxying etc. It was very thorough and to American standards. The Catalina PBY 5 with the serial number A24-10 was my charge, which was retained by me while in this squadron, although others were flown, possibly due to unserviceability of my Cat.

At this point, it might be worth recording my thoughts on some elements of operating the Catalina.

Water Handling

The Pratt and Whitney Twin Wasp R1830 engines had a tapered cylinder bore (narrowest at the tops) to allow for expansion and the bore to parallel out when at operating temperatures. Therefore, it was prudent to use reduced RPM when cold to avoid the piston jamming at the top of its stroke, thereby damaging the unit. A recommendation of 1,000 RPM or below was advised during warm up, if possible, in cold conditions.

Once again, the Pratt and Whitney was an excellent power unit, extremely reliable, and efficient. On the Cats, engine life, between engine changes, was 1,000 hours. Some of our engines were on their third life and as good as the day they started. The squadrons insisted on the return of their engines after overhaul, for occasionally ex-Dakota engines were sent as replacements. Although these were identical, they had been flogged to destruction in these aircraft, which required numerous take-offs and, we suspected, had been subjected to poor handling. More damage is done to engines during take-offs than any period of their lives. This is borne out with modern jets where the life cycle is not based on engine hours, but number of take-offs.

Due to the closeness of the propellers to the cockpit area (flight deck), it was advised to be very wary of them when the sliding top panels were open. It was possible to lose a finger or arm if caught by a blade. A number were. It was said that one could always recognise a Cat pilot because he had a finger missing.

Before slipping moorings, it was prudent to note the position and proximity of ships, their movements, plus obstacles before informing the Flight Engineer about the sequence of engine starting. One had little control over direction with the engines, especially in strong cross and downwind taxying, as the engines were so close inboard. So, all the stops were pulled out by using all means available to control the desired direction with the additional use of the ailerons and rudder. This was common to all marine aircraft, but on the Cat it was more critical than say the Sunderland where the engines, being further outboard, gave more control of direction.

Should the port engine be required to turn the aircraft to starboard, then the Flight Engineer would wind up the port engine inertia starter to maximum, then do the same for the starboard, then back to the port to top it up and engage the clutch, hoping the engine would fire up. If it fired and ran successfully, he would then top up the starboard one to await start up from the captain and then the clutch engaged.

Should the initial engine fail to start, then the whole procedure was repeated. I think that only two shots were allowed, due to overheating, when a cooling time was observed. Normally they fired up first go.

The moorings were slipped on first light up. Hanging onto the buoy after start was frowned upon, unless necessary, because the aircraft would revolve around the buoy tangling the strops, thus giving the Marine Section the task of disentangling the lines.

The Cat did have one asset in light or no wind conditions. Once clear of obstructions, with the application of a little power on one of the engines the aircraft could be made to rotate about the inboard float (causing drag). This had the advantage when downwind of staying in or near the take-off point and not having to taxy into wind for warm up and to return to the selected take-off position.

Drogues

These were really a sea anchor. Two were carried on all flying boats and were stowed inboard when not required, attached to the appropriate fitting on the aircraft, normally aft, by lines. One line fitted to the larger opening of its conical shape and the other to the smaller through the centre. They were trailed in the water on command of the pilot to take the way off the aircraft when approaching moorings.

To 'trip', i.e. reduce this retarding effect, the other line was pulled resulting in this cone being pulled inside out. Indication by the pilot as to which or both were required was by a switch in the cockpit which operated a horn in the blister compartment where the drogues were trailed. One blast indicated port and two starboard drogues. For tripping a repeat signal was made. This horn was transferable to a fitting on the mainplane pylon when used as a foghorn when at moorings.

Engine run-ups and checks were delayed until near the take-off position to reduce overheating during a long taxy, especially when proceeding down wind.

Take-Off

The control column was held firmly back, to raise the bow, as soon as possible to reduce the spray on the windscreen, props and engine. When heavily laden, a considerable amount of water came over the bow, especially in rough conditions. Full aileron was applied to assist the trailing float out of the water and reduced to maintain the mainplane level. Rudder was applied to maintain direction. The Cat hull sat low in the water, as it was a 'single deck' aircraft. (The Sunderland had two decks with the flight deck some twelve feet plus above the water.)

On the initial stage of bringing the hull onto the planing step, copious amounts of water passed over the bows, restricting the pilot's vision. In the tropics where we operated, this salt water dried on the windscreen once on the step to gain speed. The Cat was fitted with windscreen washers and electric wipers (well before they were fitted to motor cars) but these couldn't cope with this deluge. When on the step and planing, my method to have a clear view ahead was to apply starboard rudder to skid the aircraft sideways for a moment to view the path ahead through the open side-window, then straighten it. As the Cat had a relatively flat planing surface it responded in this skateboard manner.

When aileron control was gained (around forty knots) the floats were raised. This reduced drag and also added to the wing area. Also, in heavy seas, this reduced the possibility of them being knocked off. This was one problem encountered by some Sunderland pilots. The float structure was the weakest part of this aircraft. The loss of a float on flying boats could cause it to capsize. In such an event the procedure was to turn the aircraft so that the float-less side faced up wind, with crew (and/or passengers) perched on the other wing to await the arrival of sandbags (or the like) to replace them. Quite a few Sunderlands were lost through this type of accident. The Cat's float structure was more robust and had the ability to retract. As a result, few were lost due to this feature.

Another advantage of this system was while taking-off around bends of rivers, when a straight run was unavailable, where with the floats retracted, bank could be applied to reduce skidding on the turns. It was also known for Cats to carry out circular take-offs in lakes where the straight take-off run was too short.

The mainplane was quite flexible and when the floats were retracted on a heavy aircraft, they disappeared out of view of the pilot's position, to reappear when the aircraft became lighter with the consumption of fuel and shedding of bombs.

Cruise

With a full load of fuel (1,450 gallons) and bombs (2,000lbs plus) the Cat's endurance was around twenty-four hours, cruising at ninety knots. On bombing missions two-thirds of the fuel was consumed on the way out and one-third while returning. With this load it was difficult to clear 1,000 feet in the first couple of hours in tropical temperatures. We seldom flew much higher, except when on bombing and clearing the mountainous regions of New Guinea.

Bombing runs were normally made at around the 4,000 to 5,000 feet mark. The Twin Wasp engine carburettor control had five selections – Idle, Cutoff, Auto Lean, Auto Rich, Emergency Rich – and by moving the lever slightly forward from the Auto Lean setting the mixture was leaned off manually. By so doing a better fuel consumption could be attained. Care had to be taken not to exceed cruise cylinder head and oil temperature limitations.

Communication Between the Engineer and the Cockpit

The Flight Engineer's position was in the wing pylon, where apart from the normal instruments, it contained fuel flow meters and the carburettor mixture controls. There was no forward vision but a small window either side gave a view of the underside of the engines and floats. The visual communication consisted of two identical panels. One on the pilot's control column yoke – this was in the shape of an elongated 'U' section bar that extended across the cockpit and to which was fitted the two pilots flying control wheels, the ignition switches, propeller de-icing flow control and one of the signalling switch boxes. The other panel was fitted in the engineer's compartment.

Of course, there were the normal intercommunication connections at each crew position. Each box was fitted with nine switches, below each was an illuminated panel indicating its function. From left to right they read: Raise Floats, Lower Floats, Full Rich, Auto Rich, Auto Lean, Stop Engines, Recall, Inter Com. and Secure.

The switches were two-way. Say, for instance, the pilot required Auto Lean, he would switch on the appropriate switch, which would illuminate the appropriate panel light on both panels. When the Flight Engineer had carried out the action, he switched the light off by operating his switch in the opposite direction. It saved both any confusion when using the intercom and the handling a microphone during the busy take-off period (as an example).

The operation of raising or lowering the floats was normally by an electric motor, but a manual system was incorporated in case of failure. Also, as explained later, should the aircraft be landed with the floats retracted, it was prudent, due to the excessive load on the motor, to wind them down by hand.

Handling in the Air

The Cat was a stable beast in the air and reasonably manoeuvrable. On training, stalls and stall turns were practised. The rudder and elevator, I would consider, are a little heavier than the Sunderland. Exercises were carried out to impress on us the instability fore and aft if more than four people occupied the blister compartment, which caused the tail plane to stall.

An Elsan toilet, or 'can', was fitted to the aft section of the port blister. The condition of its employment was that the user cleaned it out at the next stop. A 'pee' tube was also located in the same area. The outlet was just forward of the tunnel hatch.

This hatch was situated on the lower section of the aft hull. Here there were fittings for a 0.30-inch Browning machine-gun, a bracket for mounting a camera and another for the drift sight. Normally it was closed and opened only when the navigator required to take a drift sight. Many was the time when a navigator disappeared into this area to take a drift at night and failed to notify the crew. With this hatch open the slipstream was sucked into this compartment and if someone happened to use the 'pee' tube at this time, the navigator got the lot!

The guns fitted, apart from the tunnel one, were a single .300 Browning in the manually operated nose turret, with a double-mounted .303-inch Vickers in each of the blisters. Later versions sported a single 0.5-inch Browning in each blister. When I took over A24-10 at Rathmines it was fitted with single .303 Vickers web belt machine-guns of First World War vintage in the blister positions. They jammed after a few shots were fired. No way was I going to accept this obsolete equipment, especially as the Vickers .303 'K' gun was available at this base. After much hustle the desired equipment was installed. As it turned out, we never fired a shot in anger.

Also fitted in the Cat were four bunks, an electric hot plate for cooking and an Auxiliary Power Unit (APU). The APU provided electrical power to augment the small capacity batteries on start-up and provide power when the engines were not running. While on this subject, when engine revolutions fell below 1,700rpm, their generators 'dropped off line' so 1,700rpm was considered the minimum. If a further power reduction was required, then the throttles were reduced to the required setting. Some APUs were fitted with a bilge pump and a fuelling pump.

Perhaps the greatest asset in the Catalina was the Sperry Auto Pilot. It was of pre-war design and well proven. In contrast to the Farnborough unit fitted to the Sunderland, it was a gem, far more sophisticated and reliable. With the long hours flown on our operations it took most of the workload off our shoulders.

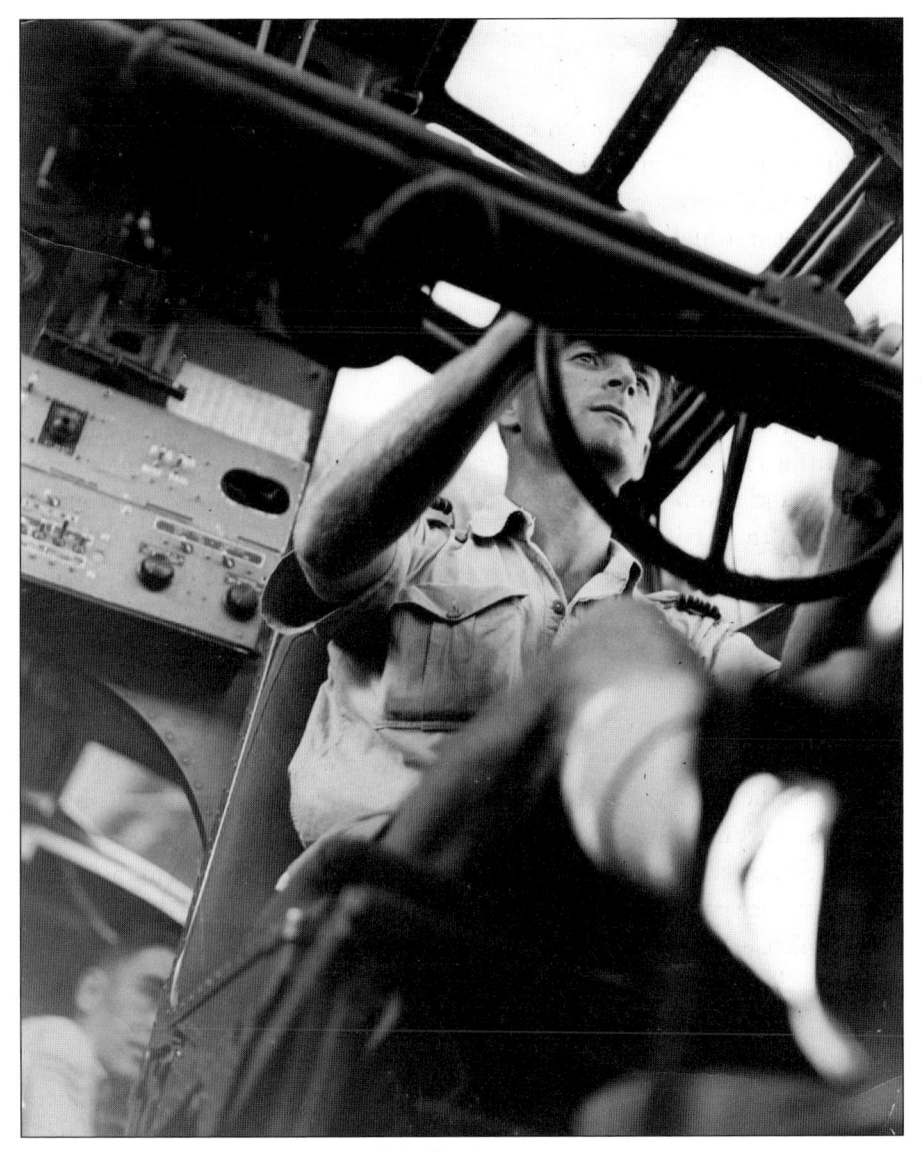

Looking up at the pilot's seat in one of the Catalinas.

On anti-shipping and anti-submarine patrols the bomb load was eight anti-submarine bombs strung under the inboard main planes. With bombing missions, the norm was eight general purpose bombs fused nose and tail with a 'Grass Cutter' extension fitted to the nose fuse. This consisted of a two-foot metal rod attached to the nose fuse. The other end was fitted with a flat disc.

As most targets were on sandy islands and between coconut trees, if a normal bomb arrangement was used then the bomb would penetrate the sand to blow a large hole in the surface. With this modification the bomb exploded above

At the controls of a Catalina.

ground and hopefully destroyed a large area, hence the term 'Grass Cutter'. The total weight of these bombs was 2,000lbs.

In addition to this we carried twenty 20lbs fragmentation bombs and twenty 25lbs incendiary bombs. My armourer had his own device whereby he scrounged Mills bombs from a local Army unit and tied tennis balls to the pins. These were supposed to bounce when hitting the ground extracting the pin. No doubt it kept him happy.

Self at the navigation table in a Catalina.

The final addition to our armament were numerous empty beer bottles. Someone in the squadron found that by fitting a razor blade a certain distance into its neck, it would produce more noise on its way down.

Apart from the 250lbs bombs carried under the main planes, the other bombs were stowed inside the aircraft and dispatched through the blisters by hand.

The gunner's position in the starboard blister on our Catalinas.

Sergeant Darcey, our Armourer, at the machine-guns in the port blister of A24-10.

As the intention on some raids was to keep the Japanese out of bed all night, when the United States Army Air Force (USAAF) medium bombers would attack at dawn, these were ideal. This all added up to grossly overloaded Cats.

I remember that one afternoon while waiting on moorings for our turn to depart, the mission being to bomb a target in the Solomons, one of the skippers, trying to go one better, loaded up with sixteen 250lbs bombs. He took off from the Cairns River out to sea. He disappeared over the horizon still on the water,

Bobby Cox, my Flight Engineer, in the galley of a Catalina.

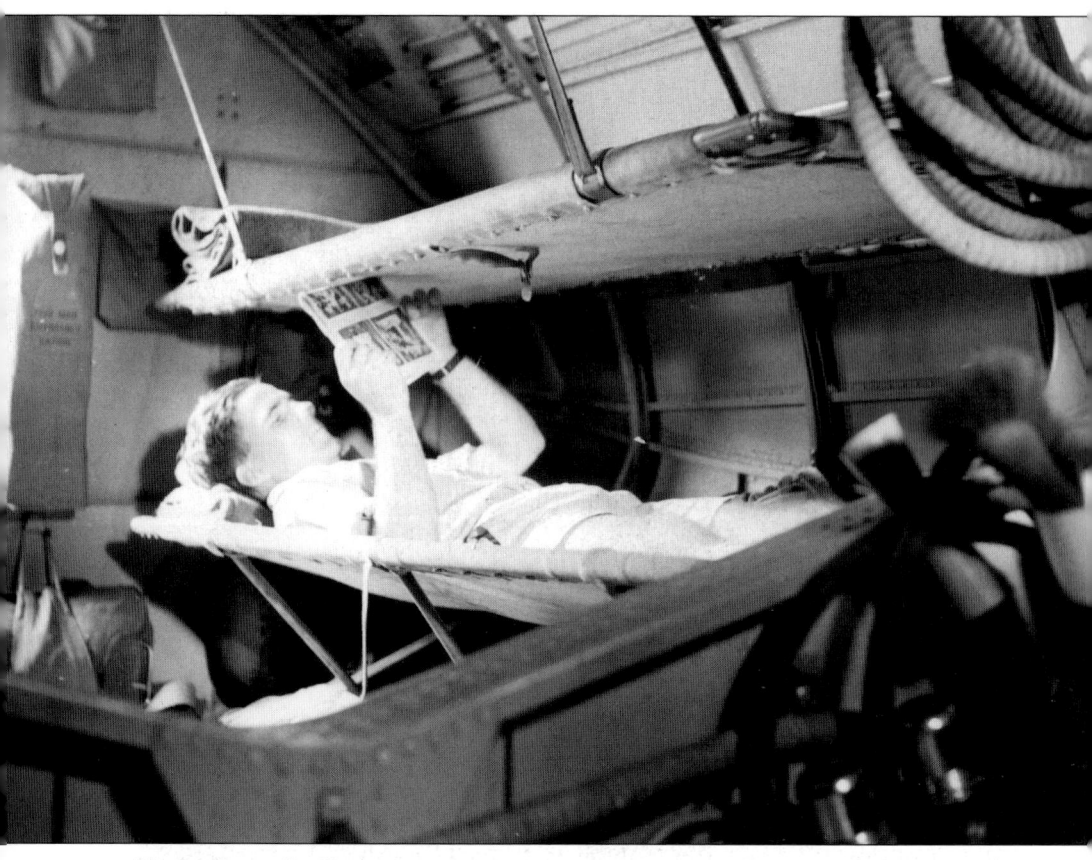

The bunks in a Catalina.

only to reappear sometime later, still on the water. The extra eight bombs were off loaded before he made a successful attempt. One could imagine the thrashing he had subjected his engines to.

Landings

Glide approaches were the norm in daylight, but glassy calm conditions required a powered approach until touchdown. This was a safe method, for it was difficult, if not impossible, to judge one's height from this surface. The same was carried out with night landings. The routine was to set the engine revs at 2,300rpm with fifteen-inch/HG of manifold pressure (boost). This would maintain the aircraft, at a reasonable landing weight, in the landing attitude at around sixty-five knots. The fifteen-inch/HG was a datum, and more power was required if heavier or less if lighter. It was a case of suck it and see.

The Flying Cats 185

The Radio Operator's position in my Catalina.

Aviation Gremlins, imagined and made in Plasticine by Self at the RAAF's Rathmines OTU sometime in 1943 or 1944. Plasticine was provided to plug bullet holes in flying boats to make them watertight on landing.

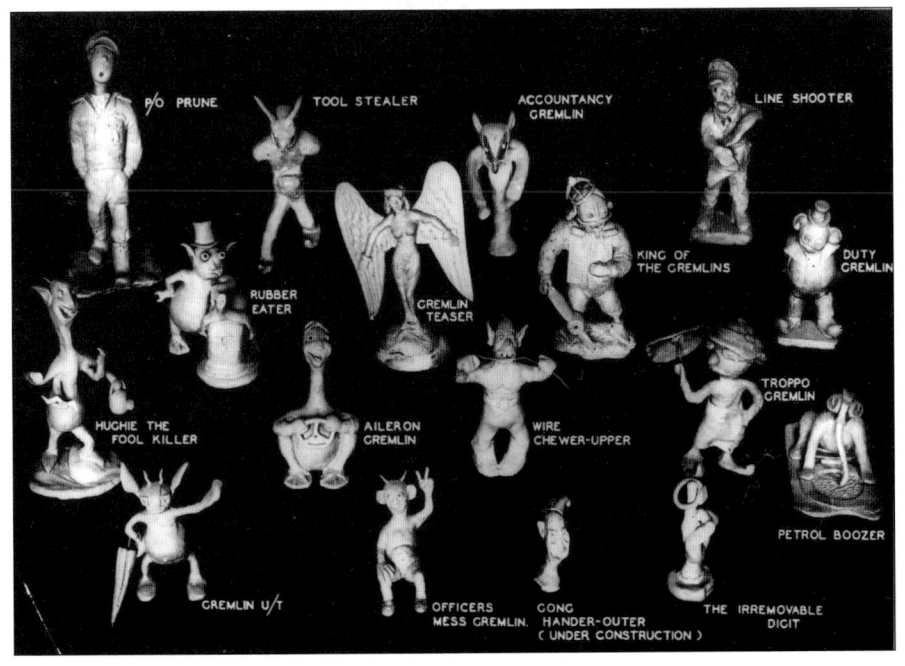

By approaching the flare path from a reasonable distance downwind one could judge the approach slope (glide slope) from the distance of the flares apart, e.g., if the flares appear bunched together you were too low, and vice versa. By applying or reducing the power and maintaining the sixty-five knots the aircraft responded by climbing or descending. Another suck-it-and-see situation.

The rate of descent datum was 200 feet/minute. With all this observed then as the aircraft was in the landing attitude and assisted by the Ground Effect (cushion of air between the aircraft and the water) it would carry out a satisfactory landing. As speed was reduced the control column was eased back.

Due to the induced drag of the water, the landing run was short. The floats, of course, were lowered on the landing check.

Another variation was used when landing in heavy seas and swell conditions. The power was set up as above and the aircraft flown at approximately thirty feet along the swell and as near into wind as possible, to await the appearance of a reasonably smooth area. The floats remained retracted to prevent them being damaged or lost on impact with the surface. A certain amount of anticipation was required for the next move.

When this relatively calmer area appeared, the throttles were 'yanked back' and at the same time the control column pulled hard back. Correct timing was required to lob in this area. The aircraft would immediately stall to firmly 'stick' to the surface. The landing run was extremely short, perhaps three times the length of the aircraft or less, depending on wind direction. One wing would drop into the water to be supported by the retracted float. This was then wound down by hand (both floats) and we became level again.

If this method was used to land in a restricted area during calm conditions, then anticipating contact with the surface the control column was shoved fully forward on contact to prevent it becoming airborne again. The impact was fairly severe and occasionally plates were buckled and rivets sprung. This was part of the training program and seldom used in earnest.

Approaches and Landings at Night

These were also practised without the advantage of a flare path. Landing lights, as mentioned before, were not used. The power, speed, rate of descent and attitude were set up as above and the aircraft flown on instruments until it came in contact with the water, when throttles eased back, together with the control column, as the speed decayed. Contact was indicated by the drag tending to pull the bow down and the sound of the water passing along the hull bottom.

This method was used when landing in hostile territory, say to take in supplies or evacuate a party of Commandos. They lit a fire on the beach for identification, but it also gave the pilot something to aim for. On take-off a star was selected and aimed for. All required fine judgement, skill and experience.

From this you may gather that the Cat was versatile and a wholly reliable beast. So, after five weeks of training at Rathmines, plus four convoy and anti-submarine patrols, we set course once again to the war. I left Rathmines on 24 June 1942, being posted to No.20 Squadron, then based at Cairns, a city in tropical Far North Queensland.

Chapter 14

Supply Drops

There were two Catalina units based at Cairns. Aside from No20 Squadron, the other was No.11 Squadron. It was difficult to know where one finished and the other started, for we all mucked in together, sharing the same facilities and aircraft. I still can't remember who was in what squadron. They were a great bunch and many a happy time was spent in their company. A number were ex-No.10 Squadron, but most had not been based overseas. All worked hard and played hard.

Our operational base was Cairns, but the maintenance base for major overhauls was at Bowen some 280 miles to the south. There was no slipway at Cairns, but one at Bowen. At Cairns we operated out of the river and the accommodation was in commandeered houses. Being married, we settled in a hotel.

A picture of the War Memorial in Cairns, with the Imperial Hotel beyond. This is the only Australian soldier known to turn his back on a pub.

For some reason we were routed via Gladstone to Bowen. It took two days to reach Cairns.

My first operation was on the night of 4 July 1942. Our instructions were to bomb Lae, a Japanese-held base on the north side of New Guinea. It turned out to be a rude awakening for them.

After seven hours, which included struggling over the mountains of New Guinea, a pass was made over Lae at 2,000 feet. The city was covered in cloud and all appeared peaceful. As I discovered later the Japanese never fired back unless someone disturbed them. My navigator who had been in the squadron for some time suggested we do a low-level attack. He, of course, was responsible for aiming and dropping the bombs.

So down to 500 feet we went, approaching from the sea. As we crossed the coast all Hell broke loose as the enemy anti-aircraft guns burst into life. It was very spectacular, if one views it in that light, but to the uninitiated (myself) appeared to be unhealthy.

After extracting ourselves from this inferno the navigator broke the bad news that he hadn't dispatched the bombs, as he didn't see a suitable target. This was no high-speed bomber but a Cat struggling along at a mere ninety knots. We were fortunate not to have been hit. I had lost interest in this low-level stuff, so climbed above the cloud to aim in the vicinity of the gun flashes and exploding bombs being dropped by the other, now arriving, Cats. This round trip took fifteen hours.

The remaining days (nights) of the month were spent on anti-submarine, convoy and bombing missions, mostly to the north of New Guinea. I clocked up a total of 105 hours for that month.

August brought a mixed bag of a convoy duties, bombing Salamau, a return bombing of Lae, a search for the USS *Jarvis* (not found) and a number of reconnaissance searches for the Japanese fleet off the eastern end of New Guinea, totalling 124 hours that month. September brought a similar pattern, with four bombing trips to Buka Passage, on the northern tip of the Solomon Islands, four convoys, off the eastern tip New Guinea, and two reconnaissance sorties hunting for the Japanese fleet off to the east of New Guinea. In this way, I clocked up 184 hours for September.

As A24-10 was due for a complete overhaul, we set course for the overhaul base at Lake Boga, to where it had been transferred from Rathmines. This was a purpose-built depot for servicing all the flying boats then operated by the RAAF and some Australian-based American flying boats, including the USAAF's or United States Navy's Catalinas, Martin Mariners, and even the odd Douglas Dolphin amphibian. This lake was off the Murray River, which is the border of New South Wales and Victoria, near Swan Hill. It was well away

Pictured at RAAF Cairns after a debriefing following a bombing run against Japanese positions at Buka in 1942. I am second from the left.

One of the RAAF's Douglas Dolphins, in this case with the serial number A35-1.

A Martin PBM Mariner, that with the serial number A70-5, of 40 Squadron RAAF during 1944.

Martin PBM Mariner A70-11, in flight circa 1944.

My Catalina, A24-10, which was nicknamed *Dagwood*, during maintenance.

from any interference by the Japanese. Having delivered A24-10, I disappeared up to Sydney to have some leave and await a collection date.

On 1 October 1942 my promotion to Squadron Leader was announced. So, on 25 November 1942, after a couple of test flights and the repair of the bottom of the aircraft, caused during launching down the slipway when a submerged steel section of the coffer dam used to construct the slipway hadn't been removed was hit, leaving an eight-feet tear along the hull bottom, we sailed off once again to the war.

On the way to Rathmines to refuel for the leg to Cairns we were diverted to Jervis Bay, just south of Sydney, to discover we were to carry out torpedo dropping trials. Airborne torpedo drops by Cats had been abandoned by the United States Navy during the evacuation of the Philippines some time before, as being impractical. They found the slow Cat a good target for the Japanese and the torpedoes 'broached' i.e., 'porpoised', which upset the gyros etc., and therefore useless.

Some people never learn or read reports, so who were we to complain. As the Beaufort torpedo training unit was based nearby, no doubt they had resurrected it. Four days and as many drops were spent there and they seemed satisfied with the results.

So, at Jervis Bay we were instructed to carry out a torpedo trial in conjunction with the RAAF's Training Unit at nearby Nowra, which had the Australian-built Beauforts. The torpedo was attached to the port bomb rack and on taxying it was evident all was not well. The weight of the torpedo (around 2,000lbs) caused the port float to almost submerge, and on slipping the buoy, the Cat rotated round this float. After some manoeuvring the aircraft was coaxed away from this obstacle, for it was determined to ram it each time we came around.

An attempt to take-off into a ten-knot wind and slight swell with asymmetric power, maximum starboard rudder, full aileron and trim tabs still resulted in the aircraft veering to port. The take-off had to be abandoned to prevent a water loop.

It was then decided to start off downwind, hoping that by the time the Cat had water looped 180 degrees, it would be into wind at sufficient speed to correct the swing and get the port float out of the water, albeit with full aileron and half rudder trim. It flew reasonably well with these settings. This method was used on subsequent trials.

The RAAF did carry out two drops in earnest, but both were failures. The first was with two American torpedoes (which would not have posed the problems encountered above) and was launched, at night, on a Japanese ship in the Celebes. The torpedoes broached in the shallow water and simultaneously the aircraft was hit by ground fire. The main tanks caught fire; the engines stopped and the aircraft stalled into the water. Only one person survived. One other attack by two Cats on shipping at Sumba also failed as the torpedoes again broached in the shallow water, but both aircraft survived. The Cats reverted to mine laying, which was their main task at this time (1943) and to the end of the Pacific War (from Darwin).

With our torpedo trials complete, we departed for Rathmines. However, during this short hop A24-10's starboard engine developed problems, which took four days of test flying to sort out. Then it was off to Cairns, via Bowen, arriving on 8 December 1942.

It was back to the grind, the first patrol following the very next day. During a patrol on the 11th the starboard engine played up again which necessitated our return two hours earlier than intended. These patrols were known as 'Milk Runs', and the buoy-to-buoy times were a shade over twenty hours.

A24-10 during torpedo trials at Jervis Bay.

The flight to the datum point, ten miles south of the Japanese held base of Gasmata, which was situated around half way along the south coast of New Britain, took six hours and the night was spent flying a Creeping Line Ahead search to the west up to the Vitiaz Strait – 180 miles as the crow flies between the western end of New Britain and northern New Guinea – and return, searching for Japanese supply ships and submarines. The latter were also being used to supply these isolated enemy bases.

The Cats had a basic radar and carried eight anti-submarine bombs. These patrols were carried out at night, starting around dusk so as to be well clear of the danger area by dawn. We never stayed in this area in daylight due to the

Japanese Zero fighter opposition. At ninety knots we wouldn't have survived an attack, though it was seldom anything was sighted.

The wooden sampans generally used for supply by the Japanese only operated at night, allowing them to 'hole up' during the day. As they were constructed of wood, which gave no return signal to radar, they were virtually impossible to locate. I only found one submarine and bombed a ship by using radar. This reported damaged the following day, but it was more chance encounter than good management.

After a couple of test flights and trying to rectify A24-10's engine, we proceeded to Bowen for an engine change. We suspected that this one was an ex-Dakota unit.

On the 26th (our next Milk Run) this replacement gave trouble, which required a diversion, after sixteen hours to Milne Bay, at the eastern end of New Guinea. The engine was 'botched up' to get us in the air to return to Cairns on one engine. From there it was back to Bowen for yet another engine change. This brings my story up to the end of December 1942.

January 1943 was a busy month as far as flying was concerned. It appears from my records that A24-10's engines were still playing up and some time was spent on test flights and running in engines. However, three convoy patrols, three Milk Runs and one supply drop were flown.

We arrived back from Bowen in a different Catalina – A24-30. Due to its problems, the old A24-10 wasn't declared fit until the 25th, and, even then, it required three test flights before acceptance.

On arrival back at Cairns on New Year's Day, we were detailed to do a Milk Run that same evening, departing some four hours later. On return from the datum off Gasmata, a signal was received to land at Oro Bay at Buna, situated on the northern coast of New Guinea opposite Port Moresby, to pick up Flight Lieutenant Hemsworth who was badly injured. At this time, Buna was on the front line of the campaign to drive the Japanese up the coast after the Kokoda Trail (from Port Moresby to Buna) battle.

Hemsworth was the only survivor of three Hudsons being used to evacuate wounded from there to Moresby. That morning they had taken-off from the strip at Buna when they were 'jumped' by Zero fighters – all three shot down, complete with the wounded. Hemsworth was wounded and the rear gunner killed, with the aircraft left well alight. To obtain some protection, he flew down to the small harbour to seek covering fire from some American ships occupying this area. However, mistaking him for the enemy, they turned their guns on his stricken Hudson, forcing him to crash land in the sea.

The smoke was so intense in the aircraft that Hemsworth opened the sliding top of the cockpit so that he could raise himself to look above the windscreen to have a clear view. Opening the hatch vented the internal smoke through this gap and further restricted his view and, of course, sucked the flames through as well, causing him severe burns.

Executing our rescue mission, expecting fighter opposition we crept in at sea level to lob in the small harbour. The crew were left aboard with instructions to push off if there was any sign of activity, while I went ashore to the casualty area some miles into the jungle to see what could be done.

Ongoing ashore, the first person I met was an old friend and neighbour who was in the Army Medical section. He was a Seventh Day Adventist, who by belief couldn't volunteer for active service, but was up there in the front line doing his part. I hadn't seen him for over six years. He said that one of my brothers was around and he would try to let him know of my arrival.

My brother, Roy, was there on my arrival back. I hadn't seen him for five years either. What a surprise in this remote area. Roy was an official war artist. My younger brother, Frank, was also an official war artist. He was discharged due to war wounds and re-joined the 7th Division as their official war artist. He once told me that out of the 6,000 7th Australian Division troops who fought the Kokoda Trail campaign, only 600 returned.

However, I was whisked off to the Casualty Unit, met the American surgeon who said that the patient was so badly injured and burned that it would be unwise to move him. I was taken to him swathed in bandages and he insisted on coming with me. So, he was bundled onto a stretcher to be loaded aboard. It was a low flight until well out of range of enemy activity when we climbed to clear the dividing mountains to Port Moresby where he was taken ashore.

I met Hemsworth years later when he was a captain with Qantas.

From Port Moresby we plodded our weary way back to a couple of quiet Cairns Brewery lagers and bed. I estimated that we were out of bed for thirty-six hours between leaving Bowen and arriving back at Cairns, and that doesn't include the time spent between getting out of bed and take-off from Bowen.

The remainder of the 139 hours flown that month were two Milk Runs, one convoy, a number of engine tests on Catalinas A24-2, A24-4 and A24-16, plus the supply drop to Coast Watchers on the east coast of Bouganville, the northern island of the Solomon group.

Supply Drop Operations

The early warning system in the war around the Solomon and New Guinea area was dependent on volunteers from the European planters and the like who knew the areas and more important those local natives who could be trusted. The bulk of the native population in this area intensely hated the Japanese and were loyal to the British and Australians. The Coast Watchers, as they were referred to, had one key piece of equipment, a portable radio which was used to report Japanese movements, including their aircraft. This information was transmitted by Coast Watchers' mobile radio units back to the US forces or the Australian base.

Constantly pursued and hunted by the Japanese, these small units were always on the move. Many were caught, to finish their days at the end of a Samurai sword. United States Navy submarines generally supplied the Coast Watchers with the necessary items and also evacuated rescued airmen etc. At times this was not possible, so we were called in.

Our loads normally included rice, kerosene (to operate the generator for the radio) and anything else required. These articles were put into jute sacks and were well padded. No parachutes were fitted, for these bags landed in thick undergrowth. The interiors of our Cats were crammed full of these items, and as normal the aircraft was well over maximum take-off weight.

We also loaded up with a few 250lbs bombs. Some of these trips took well over twenty hours to complete. A transit refuelling stop was made at Milne Bay at the far eastern end of New Guinea and we set off into the darkness to the drop point.

Having reached the area, we normally dropped a few bombs on the nearest Japanese base to give the impression that this was our objective. Then we would go down to sea level to approach the drop area. The Coast Watchers would light a fire in the jungle to identify their position and we then offloaded all the goodies. We usually had to make numerous runs in the darkness at tree top level.

These operations were a bit dicey. Having shed our load, we would creep out to sea regaining height to return to our initial bomb target to drop the remaining bombs and return to base some 1,000 miles away. We only lost one Cat on these operations. It ran into a hill on overshoot. I think two crew survived to be evacuated by submarine.

Normally when on operations the routine was to report at the Ops Room for briefing and pick up charts, code books, etc., about two hours before take-off. On bombing trips, for instance, take-off was around mid-afternoon, having risen say at around 08.00 hours. Transport would take us to the Marine Section to embark by launch to our aircraft, where the basic crew had prepared the aircraft. We then waited for our turn for departure. Normally, I think, there was a half hour break between aircraft. It was a long haul from take-off to cruise altitude of 1,000 feet. The mainplane bent so much with overloading that one didn't see the retracted wing tip floats till the following morning after dropping our load.

The time taken to reach the target determined our time over the target. Mostly, one could bet on a twenty-hour trip.

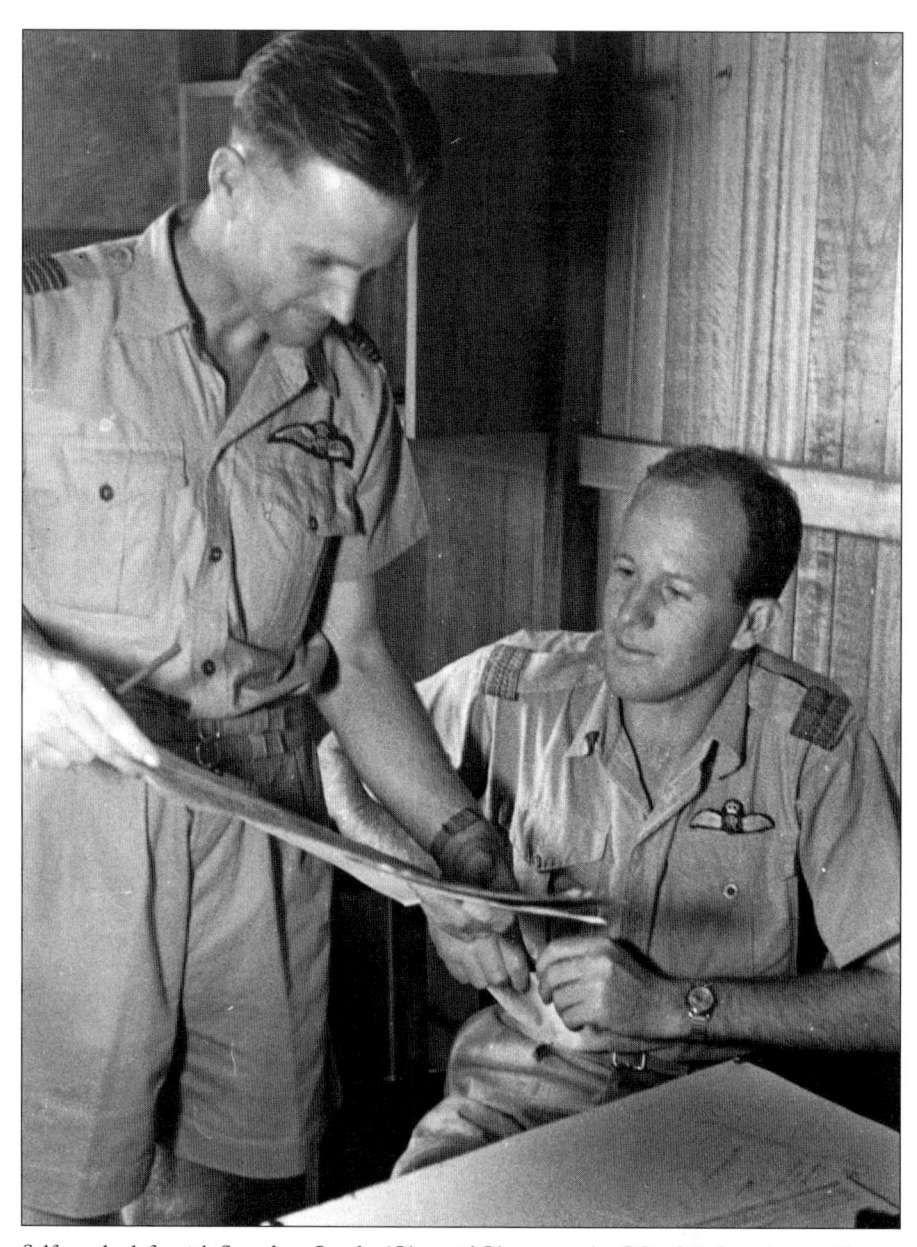

Self, on the left, with Squadron Leader 'Chappie' Chapman, the CO of 20 Squadron at Cairns. Chapman was lost off New Britain on 9 March 1943. It is thought that a parachute flare in his aircraft ignited whilst a fuse was being set.

On arrival back at base the three flight deck crew (captain, second pilot and the navigator) went ashore to be debriefed and to a well-earned rest. Overall, from Ops Room to Ops Room, our 'day' ran into twenty-four hours. It could be longer or shorter. My longest buoy-to-buoy time was twenty-five hours plus.

Our basic crew (two engineers, two wireless operators, an armourer, one rigger) remained on the Cat to tidy up, refuel and oil check, and complete any general maintenance required. Bigger jobs were done by the ground crew or left until they had had a rest. Rearming was carried out by the ground crew armament section. As Cairns did not have a suitable slipway, aircraft with serious damage had to be flown to Bowen, some 200 miles to the south for beaching and repairs.

February brought another spate of engine problems with A24-10 and it wasn't until the 14th that we got back to operations. The 14th and the 18th produced bombing trips to Kahili, and the 19th to Ballali, all in the Solomons. We seem to have started a fire at the latter. The following two were Milk Runs followed by a convoy on the 27th, giving a total month of 121 hours flying time.

My Sunderland 'tour' had finished with some excitement, and this Catalina tour was no different.

On 1 March 1943, we flew via Milne Bay westwards to the Vitiaz Strait before heading out into the Bismarck Sea. Our task was to search for the Japanese fleet reported to be en route to re-supply Lae and reinforce their troops fighting between Buna and Lae. This group consisted of three cruisers, four destroyers and fourteen merchant vessels. We searched all night in tropical storms but without a sighting.

There are numerous islands in this area and our primitive radar was unable to distinguish ships from islands. Most of the time we were flying in heavy rain and turbulence. The round trip took 25.05 hours, by far my longest. We saw the sun come up twice on that one.

All of these ships were sunk by the RAAF and the USAAF three days later, on 4 March, with the loss of a division of Japanese troops. This was responsible for the initial retreat of the Japanese.

On the evening of the 9th, as duty crew, we were called out to search for one of our Cats, which had sent an SOS. From the time the message was received, it was estimated that the stricken aircraft was around the start position of the Milk Run, ten miles off Gasmata. Apart from his call sign and the SOS nothing further was received.

As it was expected to be an air sea rescue job, the bombs were offloaded. At midnight, soon after the call, we took off for this position. As we approached New Guinea a diversion signal advised us to land at Milne Bay to await further orders. We arrived around dawn to spend the rest of the day awaiting further orders. After our departure from Cairns someone must have realised that we would be in this hostile area off Gasmata in daylight and at the mercy of Zero fighters. We would have been 'Cats meat', as the saying goes. Hence, I suspect this diversion.

No.20 Squadron's Commanding Officer had been the captain of the missing Cat. It was never found.

We suspect, after a similar event happened some months later, that a parachute flare ignited as the delay fuse was being set for ignition. This process was normally initiated near the datum in case the flare was required to identify anything below the aircraft. This setting was normally done in the blister compartment, so that it could be jettisoned immediately should something go wrong. We will never know but, as mentioned above, another Cat experienced this happening and it set the aircraft alight. These were magnesium flares of one million candle power and impossible to extinguish. This crew managed to land the Cat at night, to beach it on a Japanese-held island. While sorting themselves out the following morning they were jumped by a Japanese Army patrol and a number of them shot. The remaining few escaped to be found by some Coast Watchers and eventually picked up by an American submarine.

Late that afternoon orders came through that we were to take thirteen Commandos to Trobriand Island where seventeen Japanese had landed off an invasion barge. The latter had survived the Battle of the Bismarck Sea. The difficulty of winkling Japanese troops out from the jungle was well known then, as it is now, and all efforts were made to dispose of them before they could get ashore.

So, having embarked these tough looking Commandos and their equipment, course was set for the Trobriands. It was reputed that the women there were the most beautiful amongst these islands.

Having arrived at the appointed mission station, this troop was disembarked in native canoes. When these husky Australian Commandos, plus their equipment, climbed aboard these unstable craft there wasn't much freeboard.

Nevertheless, we departed at 18.30 hours for Gasmata and our remaining search area. The task was continued throughout the night and the only thing sighted was a surfaced Japanese submarine heading west. As we had no bombs, the best we could do was report his position and release a parachute flare causing him to submerge. After searching for an hour after dawn off Gasmata, at 300 feet, it was prudent to get out of this area.

Shortly after a signal requested us to proceed to Islet, one of many small sand islands in the area, where an invasion barge had been reported ashore. On entering this area, we discovered the sea for miles around to be covered with the debris from the Bismarck Sea battle. Thousands of dead Japanese and wreckage covered the surface and were washed up on the shores of these beautiful coral islands. Some were still alive on wreckage, waving Japanese flags. I believe these were 'shot up' later before they could cause more problems. There was no difficulty in finding the barge amongst this carnage. The debris stretched eastwards for 120 miles, as far as Goodenough Island and some to the Trobriand Islands, as mentioned.

Being short of fuel a return was made to Milne Bay and then to Cairns. Another long haul of 41.30 hours from buoy to buoy at Cairns, having departed Cairns at 24.00 hours on the 9th and returned at 17.30 hours on 11 March. This doesn't include being out of bed up to the departure and debriefing on the day of arrival. We were all a bit shattered after that one and, as usual, quite deaf from the noise of the engines.

My last operations with No.20 Squadron were two Milk Runs, a convoy and a final trip carrying Lieutenant General Laverack and party on a tour of inspection of Horn Island, near Merauke.

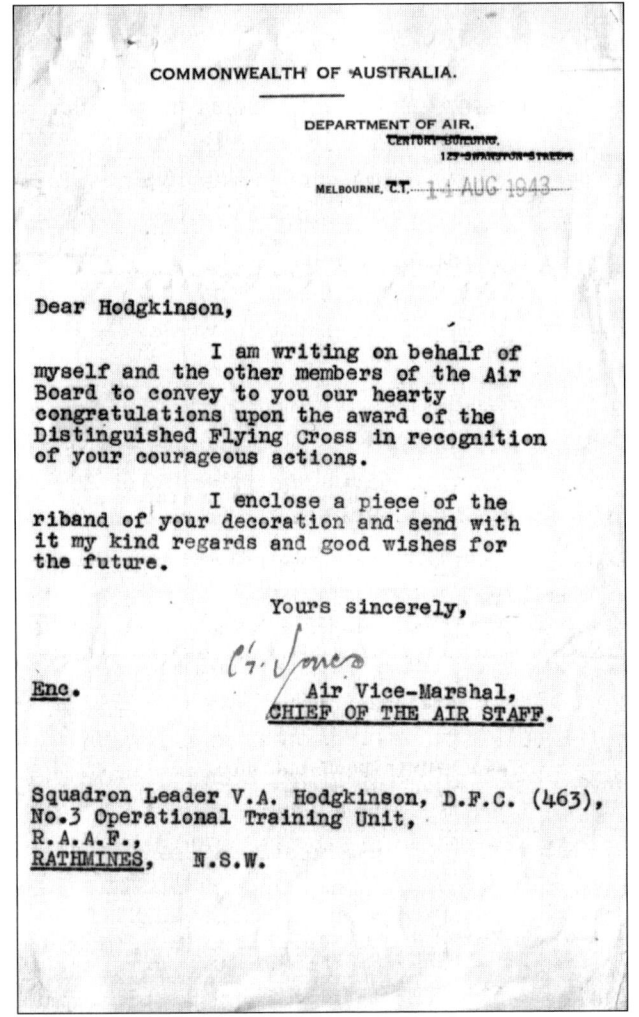

COMMONWEALTH OF AUSTRALIA.

DEPARTMENT OF AIR.
CENTURY BUILDING,
129 SWANSTON STREET

MELBOURNE, C.T. 14 AUG 1943

Dear Hodgkinson,

    I am writing on behalf of myself and the other members of the Air Board to convey to you our hearty congratulations upon the award of the Distinguished Flying Cross in recognition of your courageous actions.

    I enclose a piece of the riband of your decoration and send with it my kind regards and good wishes for the future.

Yours sincerely,

G. Jones
Air Vice-Marshal,
CHIEF OF THE AIR STAFF.

Enc.

Squadron Leader V.A. Hodgkinson, D.F.C. (463),
No.3 Operational Training Unit,
R.A.A.F.,
RATHMINES, N.S.W.

The letter that officially informed me that I had been awarded the Distinguished Flying Cross.

Prior to my departure on the 27th for this convoy patrol I was briefed to carry out an exercise with an Army searchlight unit on return after dark. Having arrived overhead at around 4,000 feet in the darkness, I waited, circling, for the 'lights to come on'. Nothing happened until my navigation lights were switched on, when they hooked on to the aircraft. Next, I did a steep turn onto the opposite direction.

The beams carried on leaving us in darkness. As would be expected, it was extremely bright in the beams. So on with the navigation lights again followed by them picking us up. We spent about an hour at this boring exercise, so deciding that as we weren't getting anywhere it was time for a beer or two, we landed.

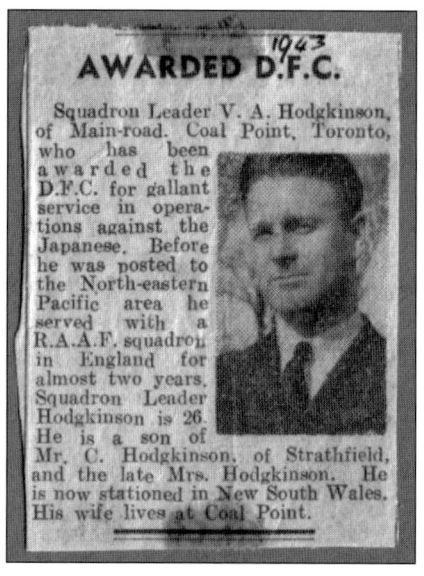

A newspaper cutting that carried the news of my DFC.

On arrival ashore, I was greeted by a most apologetic American captain. For a while I couldn't understand what he was apologising for, when I realised that an Australian anti-aircraft gun crew had fired off a shot at me, apparently bursting close to us. They hadn't been warned of the exercise. I had told my wife of this exercise and she was watching it and so thought the worst had happened to me.

The forty-four operations with No.20 Squadron amounted to a total of 227 hours. My overall total was now 3,001 hours.

Due to the loss of our Commanding Officer and, being the next senior officer, I filled this vacancy until my departure south to Rathmines. I arrived there on 3 April 1943.

On return from leave on 6 May 1943, I was posted to No.3 OTU (Operational Training Unit) Flying Boats, Rathmines as the Chief Flying Instructor, or CFI.

Chapter 15
Chief Flying Instructor

At No.3 OTU the Chief Flying Instructor's duties were to organise and detail crews for various phases of both Catalina and Walrus flying training to operational standard. Normally a pilot was not considered for the captain's course until he had served as a second pilot for 1,000 hours. There were exceptions, when if the person had a reasonable rank experience on another heavy type, this second pilot experience on the Cat was reduced.

This requirement probably accounted for fact that No.3 OTU never experienced the loss or major damage to any of its aircraft throughout the war – a remarkable record by any standards.

Dual instruction was given and the assessment of borderline pilots. The instructors were all highly experienced and a great bunch of enthusiasts. The training followed a routine of:

- Familiarisation flight.
- Slipping and mooring practice.
- Taxying in various conditions.
- Take-off and landing in various conditions.
- Stall landings in various conditions.
- Stalls and stall turns.
- Single engine procedures.
- Engine handling and cruise control.
- Effects of more than four people in blister compartment ('tail stall').
- Heavy load take-offs.
- Open sea Landings and take-offs.
- Night take-offs and landings.
- Flare path duties.

Having reached the desired standard, crews were made up of captain, second pilot, two flight engineers, two radio operators, a rigger, an armourer and the navigator. They would be grouped together and further training carried out on navigation exercises, bombing and gunnery.

The final exercise was a night trip to Middleton Reef, just to the north of Lord Howe Island, to bomb a ship wreck, photograph it (at night) and return to base. In all, this was about an eleven-hour trip.

```
.1.Allowed out of school    .2.There's death in   .3.Badge offset to    .4.This picture was    .5.This Australian   .6.Speak louder;I'm
   to be in photograph.        them thar eyes.       counteract torque    "NOT APPROVED"by       AIR FORCE palls       a trifle deaf from
                                                                          his publicity          on me;Give me         over-indulgence
                                                                          manager.               the U.S.A.F.          when a callow youth.
.1."WHAT"  (Intolerantly)  .2."ROCK OF AGES"      .3.Jack Holt fights    .4.The Queen's not     .5.Lifted off seat   .6.Spirit photo.
                              definitely a           again.                 amused.                by high pressure
                              solid type.                                                          in U/Pants.
```

An annotated group photograph of the senior officers and flying instructors at Rathmines. I am on the right-hand end of the front row.

The training Cats were all operational Consolidated PBY 5s, except for two PBY 4s. Originally these '4s' had Pratt and Whitney R1830-66 engines of 900hp fitted, but for standardisation with the '5s', were fitted with the Pratt and Whitney R1830-82 which provided 1,200hp each. The PBY 4, being an earlier model, had two dorsal hatches for the guns, but this was replaced on the PBY 5 by blisters. With the same power units, the PBY 5 was five knots faster than the PBY 4 without the blisters. It was assumed that the streamlined blisters gave a smoother airflow in this turbulent area resulting in a better performance.

By the time of my posting south from No.20 Squadron, the initial Cats were becoming time expired and required replacement for operations. Many saw out the full distance, but more Cat squadrons were required and the first of these Cats were the PBY 5A. These were of the amphibian variety. The 'A' stood for

Amphibian. With the weight of this landing gear (some 2,000lbs), they were considered unsuitable for the type of operation we expected of the Cat. The extra weight meant a reduction of fuel of this amount, approximately 280 gallons (3.5 hours) and therefore reduced range with full bomb load.

To maintain the PBY 5's performance the landing gear was removed, the nose well had a tank made and fitted into this compartment to reduce the amount of water likely to occupy this space and the main wheel wells sealed off with plates for the same reasons. Unfortunately, it was impossible to prevent water occupying all of the area not taken up by the nose tank, which made the aircraft slightly nose heavy until this surplus water drained away. With the nose gear fitted, the water content in this compartment was around forty gallons (400lbs), which affected taxying control on the water and nose heaviness during the take-off run and the initial climb, until it had drained away. Also, the wheel wells both at the bow and Engineer's compartment reduced these interior areas considerably. Of course, operating from land did not present the seaborne problems.

The 'A' Series (both 5A and the later 6A) did a sterling job on air sea rescue and communication flights, as well as used with devastating effect by the USAAF as 'Black Cats' against Japanese supply vessels. These were fitted with four 0.5-inch Browning machine-guns in the bow, which literally cut the Japanese sampans in half.

As already stated, RAAF Station Rathmines was situated on Lake Macquarie. Lake Macquarie is around fourteen miles long varying up to two miles wide. It also contains numerous bays and islands. It was estimated that landing north to south, four landings could be made on one circuit. It was virtually free of water traffic in those days. Open sea landings and take-offs were carried out in Broken Bay, twenty miles north of Sydney, where the local Auxiliary Defence Force provided safety boats. Flights to Sydney were handled at Rose Bay by the Civil Aviation Authority. This was also the Qantas flying boat base.

The units based at Rathmines were the Station HQ, which included the Marine Section, No.3.OTU (all flying boat aircrew training), No.9 Squadron, which moved to Port Stevens to the south of Nowra later, and No.1 Flying Boat Maintenance Unit, which was transferred to Lake Boga, on the Murray River in Victoria at a later date.

The Supermarine Seagull and the Walrus were virtually the same. The Seagull was the original version built for the RAAF. Twenty-four had been delivered in 1933. The RAF subsequently ordered the type, which became the Walrus. There were a few minor structural differences. They were a tough old beast, slow, but very manoeuvrable. In their way they were fully aerobatic and reputed to be the only aircraft in the pre-war RAF to be stressed to do a 'Bunt',

The seaplane and flying boat base at RAAF Rathmines. (*Courtesy of Penny Fearner*)

A post-war shot of a Seagull V, in this case the former RAAF example that had the serial number A2-4, taking-off in December 1969. Once flown by myself, this aircraft has survived and and is now destined for the Solent Sky Museum in Southampton.

i.e., an outside loop. They were also the first aircraft in the RAF to have a fully retractable undercarriage. It was one of R. J. Mitchell's many successful designs.

An additional duty of the Chief Flying Instructor at No.3 OTU was to do the acceptance flights of the Seagull/Walrus after complete overhauls by Qantas, this work being undertaken at Rose Bay, Sydney. On acceptance tests my normal procedure was to check for handling amongst other things. The aircraft was climbed to 5,000 feet over Sydney and stalled to check correct rigging and stall speed. If it dropped a wing, then rigging was suspected to be incorrect.

On one particular Seagull, it stalled at the correct speed but dropped the starboard wing every time. It was accepted, subject to further test at Rathmines. The following day, complete with three airmen who wished to come along for the ride, I climbed to the same height to carry out some more stalls. It persisted in dropping the starboard wing. I became determined to have my way and on the next stall applied full left rudder. It started to go starboard then flicked left into a spin.

In my determination I had forgotten that I was applying the flying controls in the classic position for a spin (control column fully back with full rudder). I had been flying sedate and heavy aircraft since my flying training some four years before and had forgotten this fact. So, there we were spinning down to earth – or more specifically the sea – with all the flying floppy and no control. The earth was coming up fast.

Then the old recovery action hit me – centralise the rudder, ailerons and stick hard forward. It worked and we came out at around 500 feet. I had had enough for the day, vowing I would never again meddle with the art of aerobatics.

On taxying up the slipway, I glanced at my airmen passengers. They all looked deathly white. Perhaps I had put them off flying for life?

Another perk for the CFI was to organise and operate a communication flight to Lord Howe Island, which was around 400 miles to the northeast of Sydney. This was flown approximately once a month. This small island was approximately four miles long. It consisted of two large mountains approximately 2,500 feet high to the south, where the population lived, then a low hill of 470 feet to the north. A lagoon to the east was used as an operating area for marine aircraft.

Before the war, the island depended on the Burns Philp & Co shipping service, which called once a month with necessities and shipped fish and produce plus passengers to Sydney. Due to the war this service had been discontinued, thus isolating the island. This not only stopped the small income from exports, small as they were (to pay for essential items such as oil for power, medicines, etc.,) but also the transport of islanders requiring hospitalisation, children requiring further education in Sydney, and so on.

One of our Catalinas moored at Lord Howe Island.

I can be seen standing in the centre of this photograph, taken while our Catalina was moored at Lord Howe Island.

Some twenty per cent (twenty-four people) of the entire population volunteered for service in the Australian Forces during the war. So, the island was virtually isolated.

An appeal was made to the Sydney governing body to solve this problem with the provision of a Catalina service. Lord Howe Island is governed by a trust based in Sydney and is considered a suburb of this city to this day. A Governor-Superintendent is appointed by this governing body who, in my time, was an agriculturist. The islanders specialised in growing tomatoes for seed merchants. In one year, they exported one ton of these seeds.

Being a sub-tropical island, the temperature ranged around seventy degrees Fahrenheit for most of the year and the soil was extremely fertile. Oranges of one pound weight were the norm. Prior to the war the prime export was the seed of the indigenous Lord Howe Island Palm. This palm was very popular from Victorian times up to the war as a houseplant, especially in hotels. Unfortunately, a ship was wrecked on the island and the rats, which survived, attacked the seeds. A bounty of, I think, six pence was paid for each rat tail, but the damage had been done and, in the meantime, a South American state had taken over this trade.

However, the outcome was that RAAF Rathmines was detailed to provide a Catalina once a month to provide a vital communication service. The routine was to position at Rose Bay, Sydney, embark around twenty islanders, mail and essentials and proceed to the island. The trip took around four-and-a-half hours. We landed in the lagoon. Landings and take-offs at Lord Howe were made within the period of two hours prior, and two hours after high tide, as the operating area dried out after this high tide period. There was a civil aviation radio station on the island, which sported a medium frequency beacon. This was mainly used by the Tasman Empire Air Services on their services between Auckland and Sydney, using their Short Empire flying boats.

There was no landing stage and we were taken ashore in one of their fishing boats, to be landed on the beach. The entire population was always there to welcome us. A list of the crew was given to the Superintendent, who allocated each crew member to a family for billeting. There were never enough to go around and many an argument developed on that score on the beach. The captain was the guest of the Superintendent. Their hospitality was incredible. Our two days there were taken up with picnics and fishing. In the evenings, all reverted to the Island Hall for dancing. We maintained that every time one opened one's mouth, they shoved food into it. The RAAF doctor and dentist also had a busy time.

On our return trip everyone gathered on the beach complete with hampers of fruit and goodies parcelled up in their palm leaf baskets. Our fond farewells

Passengers and crew awaiting embarkation at Lord Howe Island.

made, we departed to Rose Bay where the passengers were off-loaded and we departed back to our base at Rathmines.

The island was prone to seasonal cyclones, which produced winds of eighty mph or so. These created problems with flying boat operations, both when on moorings and during take-off and landing. This was especially when blowing from the east, for large waves came in over the reef and sometimes caused aircraft to break their moorings and be washed ashore. Some five flying boats suffered this fate. As well as these, Francis Chichester's DH Gipsy Moth seaplane capsized at moorings there during a gale in 1931 while attempting the first solo crossing of the Tasman Sea. I happened to be the second to be washed ashore in 1943.

We had collected the normal load from Rose Bay and as we approached the island the easterly wind increased considerably. This meant that our landing would be into strong winds blowing across the mountainous island, which would create severe turbulence and down draughts. I decided to attempt one pass to assess the situation and possibly return to Rose Bay if considered dangerous.

On approach I set the aircraft up in the configuration for a full stall landing. Floats up, 2,300rpm, around fifteen inches of boost and around sixty-five knots to descend to around fifty feet over the alighting area. It was quite rough and at around 100 feet we experienced a severe downdraft. Full power was applied but the aircraft still descended and with a bump we hit the water in the landing attitude.

Anticipating this the throttles were slammed shut and control column shoved fully forward. We were there! The floats were lowered and we taxied to the moorings, all intact. The sea was rough but we managed to disembark the passengers without too much trouble.

The wind persisted throughout the night. Around daybreak, I was awakened by one of the fishermen to be told that our aircraft had broken from its mooring and was up on the beach. He said that he had reported this to one of my Air Force passengers and asked if he should inform me. This officer, half asleep, told him that I wasn't to be disturbed unless it was something important, so he came direct to me.

Fortunately, it had been blown up on a sandy beach, stern first, near the Superintendent's house, and not been damaged. A hundred yards either way and it would have run up onto the rocks. The aircraft was attached to the mooring buoy lines, but the line to the mooring sinker/anchor plate had parted.

We ran the aircraft anchor as far out as possible and waited until the tide floated the aircraft then taxied it to another mooring. The wind had abated before the aircraft had been found.

After the war Lord Howe Island became a tourist attraction with the flying boats of Trans Oceanic Airways initiating the services followed by Qantas and Ansett. These services terminated when an airstrip was built across the lower part of the island, which enabled a twenty-four-hour operation, one that was not limited by the state of the tide.

The Catalina having been washed ashore at Lord Howe Island during the storm.

My Flying Boat War

The civil flying boat services began in 1947. They terminated in 1974, after some twenty-seven years. Passenger-wise, not a soul was injured or lost. But the romantic days of the flying boat had gone, being sadly missed by those who had the good fortune to have flown in them.

Fortunately, the last two Sandringham flying boats to operate this service still survive. *Beachcomber* is in Southampton Solent Sky Museum and *Islander* is, at the time of publication, in the Fantasy of Flight Museum at Polk City, near Orlando, USA.

In April 1944, six Sunderland Mark IIIs were flown to Australia from the UK, travelling via the USA. As the war was nearing its end, I suspect these six were part of a deal to replace nine originally loaned to the RAF.

Once in Australia they were stripped of their armament by Qantas at Rose Bay, to become transport aircraft for the RAAF. No doubt Qantas was selected

Islander which can be seen in the USA.

Preserved for future generations, *Beachcomber* can be seen at Southampton's Solent Sky Museum.

as it had operated the civilian version, the 'C' Class Empire Short flying boats, for many years.

In March 1944 I was posted to form No.40 Squadron, equipped with Sunderlands, at Townsville on the north-eastern coast of Queensland. As there were no flying boat facilities there it was purely an administrative gathering point for personnel, before moving to our allotted base at Port Moresby, New Guinea.

Ultimately, our first aircraft arrived when we moved our personnel and equipment to our New Guinea base. In the meantime, I had some personnel preparing the base for our arrival. By the time we arrived at Port Moresby both the Australian and American forces had moved on to Madang, leaving a hospital, transit camp and an Army works unit in their wake. All the civilian houses and other buildings had been stripped of anything useful to make packing cases, etc.

The 'town' was run by an Army Town Major, and he gave us full rein to help ourselves. The Army works unit was also cooperative and we did a deal to move its personnel back to the mainland in payment for their assistance of rolling out damaged corrugated iron sheets, providing sawn timber etc. So, we set to on creating our accommodation.

RAAF HQ were not pleased, for they had allocated us an area called 'Tin City', which lay in a malarial valley. This consisted of a few derelict tin huts and a cook house; our accommodation was to be in tents. We won an uneasy peace for they were continually pressing us to move there. It wasn't until after my posting that they enforced the move, when morale in the squadron dropped, accompanied by a rise in malaria cases.

Returning to our arrival, all of the squadron mucked in, officers and airmen alike, to build the accommodation quarters on the hill and the HQ and workshop buildings by the slipway. It surprised us that the hospital had no latrines or running water. We rectified this by building septic tanks, ablutions, electric power and a cookhouse. It was certainly much healthier up on that hill and a lot cooler.

It was agreed that our Sunderland loads would not exceed 10,000lbs on the Port Moresby sector, with a maximum of forty troops. There were no seats provided, so apart from four bunk-type seats, passengers had to make do on their packs or freight. This sector took around four hours and fifty minutes to complete.

A damaged 40 Squadron Sunderland Mk.III at Townsville – seen here in 'stealth' mode!

Having been raised, the Mk.III is secured on the beach at Townsville (Vic's wife "Terry", is on the right).

We also carried the mail. Personnel on active service were entitled to free mail. The troops soon cottoned onto this and we found that we were carrying mailbags full of coconuts. All the troops had to do was write a name and address on the coconut and put it in the post. As there seemed no point in risking our lives carrying these, we soon refused to accept them.

Personnel based at Port Moresby were entitled to one bottle of beer per week. This was dished out from the Navy stores. The Navy sent us the time-expired bottles, which had corroded crown tops, and many of these were undrinkable. This was a bit hard on the recipient for they would never replace them.

As this base was purely military, there was no means of obtaining alcohol. I believe that illicit spirits brought in by some aircraft crews were sold to the Americans for £5 a bottle. Quite a profit, when it could be bought ex-bond in Australia for 4/6d (22p). It was a court martial offence if caught, and many were. I was a member of a court martial when the Commanding Officer of

The same Sunderland is being recovered, or perhaps, more correctly, dismantled.

Another view of the badly damaged Sunderland Mk.III at Townsville.

RAAF Transport commanding officers' conference at Victoria Barracks, Melbourne, on 20 September 1944. I am third from the right.

an Australian Dakota squadron was charged with the trading of grog with the American forces. Apparently, he had not given an airman, the go-between, his agreed cut of the profits and the airman duly reported his CO.

Another incident around this time was of another Commanding Officer of a Dakota squadron who had obtained a written-off B-24 Liberator bomber from the USAAF. Having made it serviceable, he used it as his personal aircraft. One day he took off from Adelaide for New Guinea loaded with grog in the bomb bay. On take-off he operated the 'Wheels Up' switch and hit the 'Bomb Doors Open' switch by accident, thus spreading his load over the countryside.

Operating a daily service to Townsville, we were fortunate to be able to keep our bar stocks up in both the Sergeants' Mess and Officers' Mess. The understanding was that it was purely for use within those Messes and strictly adhered to. Ex-bond it cost 4/6d for Australian gin and rum and $5 for Australian

In the cockpit of a 40 Squadron Sunderland, circa 1945. Squadron Leader Smith is on the left, with Self looking up at him.

A Dutch Dornier Do 24, one of several which escaped from the Dutch East Indies and were subsequently used by 40 Squadron RAAF. I logged a couple of hours on one of these aircraft.

whisky. This was named 'Corio', after COR-10, a brand of petrol (Colonial Oil Refinery No.10). It certainly tasted like it.

In their wisdom, RAAF Headquarters allocated two crews per aircraft. I think that at this stage of the war there was a surplus of flying crew, which became an embarrassment. So, they farmed the surplus out to squadrons and other units to get them out of sight.

Another embarrassment was the generous promotion system. Provided one kept one's nose clean, promotion was on a time basis. So, with the war dragging on and casualties reducing, the show was becoming top heavy with senior officers. I had four squadron leaders as captains of aircraft who, in the order of things, only flew once a fortnight. So, they and the other twelve complete crew members had little to do between trips. As one aircraft was under overhaul at Qantas, Sydney, for around a couple of weeks, it allowed one crew unofficial leave for that period.

After much persistence, I finally managed to convince Headquarters to reduce our crew allotment to one per aircraft and the squadron leader captains, except for the flight commander, were posted. This made life a little easier for me, but, of course, some personnel were upset.

In May 1945 I had done my time and was posted to a staff course at Mt. Martha, Melbourne. I must say I found this hard going and the thought of sitting

An outdoors group portrait of the directing staff and the students of No.7 War Staff Course at the RAAF Staff School, Mt Martha, Victoria, in 1943. Left to right in the back row are: Sqn Ldr O.M. Kelsey; Sqn Ldr R.D. Baird; Wg Cdr John Edward Handbury; Captain J.H. Lukkien, Netherlands East Indies Air Force; Sqn Ldr R.M. Green; Wg Cdr Harvey Holcombe Smith; Wg Cdr L.R. Trewren; Sqn Ldr R. Widmer DFC; Wg Cdr S.W. Galton; Sqn Ldr N.M. Pilcher. Middle row: Wg Cdr S.G. Quill, RNZAF; Wg Cdr George Emile Prosser; Wg Cdr G.M. Robinson; Wg Cdr Hamilton Wellesley Connolly DFC; Wg Cdr S.W. Martin; Wg Cdr G.T. Miles; Sqn Ldr H.V. Jenkins; Wg Cdr A.E. Cook; Wg Cdr V.A. Hodgkinson DFC; Wg Cdr N.E. Morris; Wg Cdr G.J. Towers. Front row: Major W.H. Harper, AIF: Gp Capt Edwin Glen Fyfe; Gp Capt Dixie Robison Chapman; Gp Capt R.H. Sims, AFC; Air Vice Marshal William Hopton Anderson CBE, DFC, the school commandant; Wg Cdr D.L.G. Douglas OBE, DFC, the unit Commanding Officer; Wg Cdr G.V. Candy; Wg Cdr D. Ingles; Acting Gp Capt R.F.M. Green. The school's mascot, a bulldog, stands in front of the group. The school ran Staff Courses and Unit Commanders' Courses of three months and six weeks' duration respectively. (Australian War Memorial; P02352)

on my backside for the remainder of my RAAF life didn't appeal to me. Three months of this was followed by a posting to Point Cook, near Melbourne – the station where I had done my cadet course in 1939, as Senior Administrative Officer. There was little to do there for the Commanding Officer was a one-

Self – pictured at Point Cook during my time as the Senior Administrative Officer there.

man band who had been there for years. He was a nice chap, far senior to me, but still a Wing Commander, the same rank as myself. I suspect he had seen little active service and resented my presence.

The war had packed up during this period and my next posting was to RAAF HQ Eastern Area, Sydney. This was really a Group Captain's post. I was a fill-in until an officer of this rank was available. The war was over, so the main job was organising the breaking up of various units and also organising 'Loan flights'.

After the war the Government decided to raise money with the carrot of offering those who bought bonds of a certain value a ride in a destroyer, a tank or a flight in an RAAF aircraft. For the latter, the Catalina was the chosen aircraft. Working with the appropriate members of the other two forces I did the Air Force side and worked my way into doing some of the flights.

After a few months of this I was posted to the flying boat base at Rathmines as Senior Administrative Officer. It was like returning home, but the bottom had dropped out of the place. The CO was not a 'web footed' type, discipline had deteriorated, due to personnel being demobbed, and security was poor. We managed to obtain guard dogs, but the WAAFs fed them and they became useless.

Having been in the 'Loans' set-up, I suggested to Eastern Area HQ to replace the Catalinas with a Sunderland, numbers of which were now laying idle on moorings at Rathmines. Instead of the twenty-odd passenger uplift of the Cat, the Sunderland could be increased to forty. This appealed to them, and, as I was the only person available to pilot the aircraft, I spent a few weekends at both Sydney and Melbourne doing these flights. My CO was not pleased, for it meant that during these times he had to remain on the station.

Then I note that I was shuttled between Eastern Area HQ and Rathmines until I decided that I wasn't cut out to sit on my bum for the remainder of my life in the RAAF. I applied for an advertised flying job with British Overseas Airways Corporation on flying boats based in the UK. I was accepted in May 1946, being demobbed the same month.

I had accumulated 4,347 hours flying in the RAAF. Of the fifty cadets who I joined at Point Cook in January 1939, only around nine of us survived. The same applied to our senior course. I saw very few of my course members after our postings to active service. This was basically because of my posting to the UK and the fact that flying boat bases never appeared to be anywhere near land-plane bases. We lived in a different world – 'The Web Footers Club'.

Chapter 16

From Flying Boat to Boeing 707

The following account of Vic's post-war career was written by John Maynard for *Aeroplane* magazine and published in its August 2006 issue. Following an interview with Vic, John set out to explore the former's illustrious civil aviation career which, lasting from 1946 through to 1971, encompassed very different eras of air travel.

In 1946, the British Overseas Airways Corporation (BOAC) advertised in the *Sydney Morning Herald* for experienced flying-boat pilots, indicating that about 50 were immediately required. Vic Hodgkinson resigned his commission and surrendered his Service number, a notable 463! As well as his DFC he had been Mentioned in Despatches.

Having been finally accepted by BOAC, Vic and his family returned to the UK. His wife Terry, with their baby son, Robert, boarded the Union Castle liner *Stirling Castle*, while Vic was flown in a Hythe, a civil conversion of the Short Sunderland, to Poole, and thence to BOAC's London headquarters.

It rapidly became clear that this was not the best-organised recruitment exercise of all time. It appeared that far too many recruits had been brought to London, and the BOAC hierarchy was discomfited by the discovery that some lacked four-engine experience, having been Consolidated Catalina men for their entire operational service. These were promptly sent home to Australia, and the remainder were put on to a training course at Poole. This was pretty rich as far as Vic was concerned, with his 1,800 Sunderland hours, most of them in command. However, he sucked his teeth and got on with it.

Meanwhile, Terry arrived after a terrible journey by sea in a hot ship with no air-conditioning and a cabin at waterline level shared with her young son and no fewer than four nuns. The food, which was somewhere beyond disgusting, had been aboard before the *Stirling Castle* left England outward bound! Overall, the journey seemed to have deteriorated since Vic went to war in late 1939.

Training at Poole also had its moments in the hands of training captains who were recently promoted first officers, often with pre-war Imperial Airways experience which was assumed to give them a quite spurious cachet! A bleak captain known as 'Snag' undertook Vic's training and customisation to BOAC standards. He had earned his nickname from a tendency to find fault with everything and everyone, and specialised in immensely long, low, flat powered approaches occupying miles of sea and usually ending in multiple touchdowns. 'Time of landing?' he roared at one pupil, who replied: 'I've got seven here; which one do you want?' When the time came for examinations the navigation paper failed many of them, including Vic, who went on an appropriate course with Air Service Training at Hamble and thereafter passed without difficulty.

Finally, he went down the routes on Hythes as a first officer, which included services all the way down to Sydney in 5½ days, the Dragon service to Hong Kong via Karachi, Calcutta, Rangoon and Bangkok, and a route from Singapore to Hong Kong which, at the time, linked with an RAF Sunderland service to occupied Japan. Competition was provided by BOAC Avro Lancastrians, which flew from Heathrow to Sydney with nine passengers in 63 noisy hours. The Hythe was no beauty, retaining the bluff outline of the Sunderland's nose and tail turrets, but with their locations covered in sheet metal. Accommodation was for up to 24 day passengers.

Vic has endless first-officer memories of the many captains with whom he flew. Some spent most of their time socialising with passengers in the back, returning to the flight deck only to berate the crew or handle some perceived problem. One had a phobia about flying in cloud and, since much of the journey was covered at below 5,000ft, one could have some sympathy but surely not over the sea! This captain was a navigator's nightmare, as he changed course, flying hither and thither to stay in clear blue sky. He once returned from a chat to the passengers just as Vic took a chance and went through, rather than round, a cloud. The captain bounded across the cockpit to press his face against the temporarily opaque windscreen. 'Where are we, what are you doing?' he wailed at Vic, and seized the controls for the remainder of the flight.

There were captains who sought to break records, captains who could not avoid breaking aeroplanes, and captains who came within an ace of breaking their necks. All seemed to be imbued with a profound self-confidence, especially if their service included Imperial Airways time. They had much in common with clipper captains of times gone by

The passengers must sometimes have wondered just what on earth was going on. For instance, when in bad weather they spent more than a quarter of an hour circling a flashing lighthouse en route between Alexandria in Egypt and Augusta in Sicily. In fact, the two captains on board, one of whom was a passenger, were arguing about where they were, while the first officer maintained a tight orbit round the light. At issue was a fundamental decision as to whether they flew on north or south!

Another captain noted for his 'press-on' characteristics had no compunction about summoning his passengers from their over-night hotel accommodation at the most ungodly hours to catch up on lost time. Once, after an engine change, anxious to complete a test flight before embarking passengers, he opened the throttles wide, having cast off. The 'boat surged forward, only to come to an instant juddering halt owing to the storm-mooring still being firmly in place under the hull! The same man was racing across the Sind desert on the Karachi-Calcutta stage, principally to catch up and overtake the 'boat that had left an hour or so before them, when, with a massive bang, he almost literally lost the starboard outboard engine. Two valves had seized, causing the cylinder pot to blow off and detach the entire cowling, closely followed by the piston and conrod, which both thudded into the leading edge of the fin. Discretion prevailed, and they limped back to Karachi covered in black oil.

Eventually Vic was promoted captain, but first he served as a 'Temporary', meaning that he could stand in for captains who went sick or were otherwise indisposed. He recalls that this meant carrying two uniform jackets at all times and only being paid the salary when he was actually in the left-hand seat. When his 'boat time came to an end in 1950 he had amassed 3,110hr along BOAC routes to Hong Kong, across Africa, to Johannesburg and the long haul down to Sydney.

From the Hythes he had moved on to Short Sandringhams and Solents, both of which departed from the Sunderland's starkly military hull lines to assume an attractive streamlining. But the flying-boat's days were numbered, BOAC had lost interest and landplanes were clearly destined to be the future of civil aviation.

On 10 November 1950, the national airline announced the termination of all flying-boat operations forthwith. It was a sad but perhaps inevitable day. Vic looked back on 7,490hr of 'boat time.

It would be good to record that the withdrawal of BOAC's flying-boat services was hastened by the burgeoning success of its landplane operations, but sadly this was far from the truth. The British aircraft industry, for a variety of reasons born of the exigencies of war, signally failed to offer a civil transport aeroplane attractive, or even acceptable, to BOAC in the immediate post-war years. This was partly due to BOAC imposing quite unrealistic demands on British manufacturers because it really wanted to acquire established and comparatively advanced American equipment, thus avoiding the hassle of proving new designs while establishing worldwide services. The snag was that the dollar-strapped and near-terminal British post-war economy forbade the purchase of the Lockheed Constellation fleet that BOAC craved, and Avro Lancastrians and Yorks soldiered on in the absence of the Avro Tudors, which were finally rejected in 1947.

In 1948 the airline was permitted by the Labour government to buy eight Constellations, and more followed. These were joined by Boeing Stratocruisers the following year, as well as by the happy compromise of 22 Canadair C-4s, christened Argonauts by BOAC. The Argonaut was essentially a Douglas DC-4 built by Canadair and powered by four Rolls-Royce Merlin 626 engines. It was about as close to a 'British' modern long-range airliner as it was possible to get.

Vic Hodgkinson was assigned to the Argonaut fleet and immediately encountered another failure-induced situation. British South American Airways (BSAA), which had been run by Air Vice-Marshal Don Bennett, wartime leader of Bomber Command's Pathfinder Force, collapsed after the unexplained loss of two of its Tudors over the Caribbean without trace. Many of BSAA's captains and crews were absorbed by BOAC, seriously curtailing promotion prospects.

Vic was very happy from the start of his time as a first officer on the Argonaut, which was an unusually well-tried aeroplane now powered by a king among engines. It was docile, predictable, and in every sense a pilot's aeroplane. BOAC's Argonauts, among the first airliners to sport the smart white heat-reflecting

BOAC Canadair C 4 "Argonaut" 1953. Self and other crew members.

fuselage tops, plied old and hot Empire routes to Hong Kong, and on to Japan, to Nairobi, down to Cape Town, and East and West Africa, to Singapore with stops in the Middle East in India, Pakistan and Burma. Services were also initiated on the old BSAA routes to and across South America. Vic stayed with the Argonauts for seven years, sadly encompassing the period when many were hastily brought from retirement to replace the grounded de Havilland Comet I fleet in 1954. He amassed 4,000hr in the type, latterly as a captain, bringing his total hours to some 12,000.

The next phase in his career should have been memorable, but it was not. He went as a captain to the Bristol Britannia 102 fleet, and disliked the aeroplane from the start. It was, he told me, what the Australians would call a 'bag of nails'. It initially suffered chronic icing problems within its innovative Proteus turboprop engines which persisted despite radical 'cures', and ice affected other aspects of the aircraft, including the gearboxes within the hugely complex rod-operated control system. It was just too clever for its own good, and Vic is particularly scathing about those responsible for its design and acquisition. He transferred to the Comet 4 fleet after only 610hr.

He liked the Comet and, in particular, the impressive power of its four Rolls-Royce Avon engines. He did not like the less-than-adequate thrust reversal available only on its outboard two Avons, and he found the pilot's field of vision from the cockpit both distorted and restricted. Apart from these criticisms he admired its flexibility, the durability of its systems and the great strength of its undercarriage.

One night landing in a veritable deluge of rain at Baghdad particularly proved this point. He told me: 'The army had been exercising at the airport all day and tanks had deposited a mass of sand on the runway from their tracks. The rain had turned this into deep slimy mud and, after a poor visibility landing somewhat beyond the threshold of the 8,000ft runway, I began to apply the Maxaret anti-skid braking. Shortly thereafter, and at about 100kt, the Comet swung through 90° and continued on sideways down the runway. I sorted that out by violent differential braking and straightened up, only to have the aeroplane swing the other way before finally stopping.

There was no fire on the tyres, no apparent damage, but a look out of the door while awaiting the arrival of cabin stairs, bus and emergency services confirmed a runway surface more like a muddy farmyard. My cabin crew could only advise passengers to remove shoes and socks, or stockings, and roll up trousers before walking to the buses. "Buckets and spades," announced the stewardess, "are available outside". At least it lightened the atmosphere!

'I recall that the aircraft was G-APDH, a reputedly spooked aeroplane (not that I believe that tosh) which suffered a series of misfortunes before burning out in an unexplained ground fire at Singapore on 23 March 1964, in which no-one was injured.'

Vic did 2,500 Comet hours before transferring to the Boeing 707 fleet, on which he captained both Rolls-Royce Conway and Pratt & Whitney 336-powered aircraft. He was by now a senior captain, first class, and he stayed on 707s until retirement in 1971, at which point he had 19,300hr in his logbook.

Vic was in his element in the 707s. The world was his back yard; he flew passengers, he flew freight, he flew charters. As he told me: 'You name a destination, we went there.'

It was a fine way to wrap up 25 years' service with the airline. One of his last flights found him in Hong Kong, suddenly scheduled to take a 707 to Manila. On return he flew passengers to Osaka and then back to Tokyo. When he was required next to take a flight from Tokyo to London via Moscow he was conscious of not having had a great deal of sleep. He recalls: 'The journey across Russia was fraught with problems. Initially we were held well below our operating altitude by "converging traffic", and available navaids were generally not available; essentially there was just one beacon and it wasn't working. Eventually I called up Moscow for a weather report and it was abominable, so I requested an alternative and received the bland reply: "Roger" and nothing further!

'Arriving at Moscow, I found my way round the very basic approach pattern, but aborted on finals at 100ft with no visibility at all in the driving sleet. Climbing away, I demanded an alternative and was again advised that all were closed by the weather. Taking matters into my own hands, I headed for Leningrad with dwindling fuel and Moscow's cries of "Leningrad no good" ringing in my ears.

'It was more by good luck than good judgment that when I broke through the low cloud base the runway [at Leningrad] lay dead ahead, at least partly cleared of snow by Russia's very agricultural device of a jet engine on a lorry.

'There followed hours of frustration in which I negotiated with the blank-faced Russian army of bureaucrats for fuel, food for my passengers and beds for us all. We were housed and locked into an empty barrack-block with minimal facilities for the bitterly cold night. I had managed to get hit three times by a military sentry I walked past and, not surprisingly, found I couldn't sleep, and prowled round the corridors all night, my third without proper sleep.

'Next morning, I gathered up the passengers, who by now regarded me as their hero, saw them through the boarding procedures, and obtained the necessary flight clearances before settling in the cockpit to do my checks. As we finally cleared Russian airspace, I flicked the PA switch and announced: "This is Captain Hodgkinson speaking. You will be pleased to hear that we have just left Russia." They cheered us to the echo!'

Vic wrote a long report for BOAC, detailing the dangerous problems they had encountered in Russia, but it was never acknowledged, he was never interviewed, and he heard of no action ever being taken. A few months later he retired and, after bidding a fond farewell to his last crew at the end of his last flight, he refused a drink with the Chief Pilot and drove happily home to Lymington, to Terry and their family.

In retirement Vic has found great satisfaction in promoting the story of flying-boats and ensuring that their contribution to the growth of air travel is never forgotten. He worked as a volunteer in the Southampton Hall of Aviation for many years, showing visitors around *Beachcomber*, the Short Sandringham exhibited there. He has a proprietary interest in the beautiful 'boat, having fought and worked hard for its acquisition, restoration and preservation, an epic story in its own right. It was bought in 1982 by the Science Museum and the National Heritage Memorial Trust for £85,000, and Southampton City Council offered to build a museum to house it.

Then began a classic process of restoration, carried out by volunteers in often trying circumstances and involving a move from Lee-on-Solent to Southampton's Eastern Docks and on through the City to the site of the new museum, which was then effectively built around *Beachcomber*. The volunteers achieved miracles of improvisation and perfection within the fully-furnished aeroplane, in the course of which Vic added upholstery and seat cover work to his multiple skills. The flying-boat has some 19,500hr on the clock, thought to be the highest of any Sunderland type. You may even have been fortunate enough to have been shown over it by Vic Hodgkinson, and have heard at first hand his fascinating, courageous story, spiced with an endearing, very Australian, humour.

Appendix I

Plymouth Sound Notes

In my experience, Plymouth Sound was perhaps the most hazardous of areas to operate Flying Boats during WWII. It must be remembered that after the second evacuation of France to southern England – mainly Plymouth & Falmouth – Plymouth became very congested with all types of shipping, both Naval & Merchant, for the remainder of the War.

Although it did not prevent Flying Boat operations for Coastal Command from RAF Mount Batten, both take-offs & landings were restricted to areas between ships, both day and night, where both space and length of run was considered adequate. In some directions this was not possible due to obstructing hills, radio masts, etc. In fact, the only feasible runs for take-off were to the south from the Hoe to the Breakwater and parallel to the Hoe to the east of the Cattewater. Heavily laden Sunderlands required about a mile to become airborne in reasonable conditions, fully laden, a good chop and prevailing wind. Even then the rate of climb initially was more like 2-300 feet per minute. We are talking about old technology aircraft and not jets. It was a "Seat of the Pants" operation. An engine failure (or structural) could mean a write-off of both aircraft and crew. Fortunately, few occurred.

As mentioned above, after this evacuation, these ships anchored in the Sound consisted of all types, some "sported" Barrage Balloons which were "short hauled" at 400 feet…thereby adding another hazard. Nothing was lit at night due to the Blackout. Ships were never lit at night nor, I think, carried navigation Lights. So, it was a "free for all" situation.

So, what with relatively inexperienced crews, heavily laden aircraft, shipping obstructions, debris in the water from this shipping, blackout, short flare path, restricted landing & take-off runs, no brakes, the poor manoeuvring characteristics of Flying Boats in general, to mention a few of the hazards to be overcome by the skipper; <u>it amazes me & no doubt others why more accidents or incidents did not occur.</u>

There is only one other Flying Boat base, during the War, which presented similar shipping hazards that I experienced, and that was Alexandria, Egypt. This harbour, which existed behind a long breakwater, was crammed to overflowing with shipping after the evacuation of Crete. The shipping was moored north/south & the Sunderland operations were confined to an area between the two lines of merchant ships to the eastern end. There was barely enough room to turn within it. The strong prevailing northerly sea "breeze" made taxying downwind precarious as the aircraft fought to "Weathercock" into the wind. Small "Felucca" (taxis) & Naval Pinnaces appeared frequently from between the shipping to add to the congestion and hazards. It was always a relief to become airborne. Fortunately, night operations were carried out in Aboukir Bay, to the east of Alexandria where a large RAF Maintenance & Repair Station existed. This bay was where the Battle of the Nile was fought by Nelson. There were still some of the French guns lining the foreshore, after all those years.

Vic Hodgkinson. 2002.
Ex. 10 Squadron RAAF

Known Sunderland Crashes in the Plymouth Sound area 1939–45

Originally compiled by D. C. Teague, Plymouth (deceased).
Revised by W/Cdr V. Hodgkinson, ex 10 Squadron RAAF, 2002 (deceased 2010).
(Locations only approximate)

Date:	Aircraft & Details:	Squadron:
15-10-1939	N3090. Crashed on night landing Mt. Batten. Misjudged height after patrol. Crashed outside Breakwater. 4 killed.	204 RAF
27-11-1940	N9048. Destroyed in hangar in air raid by fire.	10 RAAF
27-11-1940	P9601. Sunk at moorings in same air raid.	10 RAAF
29-12-1941	W3998. Crashed on take-off. 1 killed. Struck off charge 1 Jan. 1942	210 RAF
12-11-1942	W6054. Crashed landing Plymouth Sound & sank. Struck water on aborting landing & overturned 1½ miles south of Plymouth. On ferry flight. 5 killed, not RAF.	10 RAAF
29-03-1943	Mk. III "V" of 119 Sqdn. Founded but salved.	119 RAF
20-05-1943	W3986. Crashed Eddystone Light after take-off from Mount Batten. Caught fire 15 minutes after take-off 4 miles N.W. Eddystone killing 12 crew.	10 RAAF
07-10-1943	W3993. Collided with W4024 of 10 Squadron. While other aircraft was at moorings.	10 RAAF
07-10-1943	W4024 – As above.	10 RAAF
05-01-1944	T9110. Damaged heavy landing. Plymouth Sound. Broken lost float (Port). Flying training.	10 RAAF
01-06-1944	EK574. Collided with buoy while taxying in harbour for take-off for anti-sub. patrol & sank. Crew escaped.	10 RAAF

232   My Flying Boat War

Date:	Aircraft & Details:	Squadron:
19-06-1944	JM678. Caught fire at moorings & sank, during cleaning & maintenance. 3 injured. Mt. Batten.	10 RAAF
16-09-1944	W4030. Hit Pinnace on take-off at Mt. Batten. When airborne. Damaged float.	10 RAAF
02-09-1944	DD852. Hit by ship while moored & drifted onto rocks. Plymouth Sound.	10 RAAF
12-10-1944	ML839. Sank during gale, between 05.00-07.45. At moorings with crew on board	10 RAAF
11-12-1944	ML782. 04.45 – Made heavy landing on return from anti-sub ops. Sank on landing. Blew up during salvage when Depth charges exploded. 2 crew killed on landing & 6 from salvage boat.	201/228 RAF
09-02-1945	ML829. 07.11 – Either Port Engine outer engine failed or pilot stalled aircraft on take-off for ops. Crashed & sank into anti-submarine net (boom). 2 killed, 6 injured, 3 uninjured.	10 RAAF
04-03-1945	PP138. 13.18 – Lost prop in flight-starboard inner-& ditched while on anti-sub patrol. Operating from Pembroke Dock (?)	10 RAAF

Additional Sunderland Crashes, Plymouth Sound Area (1939–45)

Compiled by W/Cdr. V. Hodgkinson.
Extracted from Aircrash Log No. 3 – Short Sunderland & Aeromilitaria, No. 3, 1979

Date:	Aircraft & Details:	Squadron:
20-09-1939	N9028 – Mt. Batten-moored London K5262 swung into aircraft during strong tides & wind.	204 RAF
13-10-1939	N9045 – Ran out of fuel near Scillies. Landed heavy seas & port float torn off. Crew saved; aircraft sunk.	204 RAF
16-10-1939	N9030 – Misjudged height on landing after patrol; crashed in Sound outside Breakwater. 4 killed.	204 RAF
25-12-1940	P9605 – Starboard float struck buoy whilst taxying.	10 RAAF
10-01-1941	P9600 – 18.05 Struck submerged wreckage, on alighting on flare path.	10 RAAF
27-08-1941	P9604 – Forced landing Coverack Cove, near Falmouth, Cornwall.	10 RAAF
21-12-1941	W3998 – Error of judgement; crashed in sea 200 yards from Breakwater Fort. Killing 11 & injuring 4.	201 RAF
13-01-1942	W3985 – 03.00, Struck ship which had dropped anchor in gale.	10 RAAF

Plymouth Sound Notes

Date:	Aircraft & Details:	Squadron:
01-03-1942	W3999 – 15.40, aircraft fell heavily due to sudden gust of wind on landing. Port float damaged. On test flight of automatic pilot	10 RAAF
28-04-1942	T9109 – 15.00, Swung into wall, while taxying gusty wind.	461 RAAF
22-05-1942	W4004 – Forced landing due bad weather; starboard float ripped off in heavy swell	10 RAAF
27-05-1942	W4020 – Aircraft blown from moorings in Scilly Isles onto rocks.	10 RAAF
15-07-1942	W3985 – Refuelling barge drifted into aircraft.	10 RAAF
04-09-1942	DV966 – 11.20, Struck naval boom while taxying during taxy test.	204 RAF
28-11-1942	W6015 – Aircraft went missing at 23.15; 12 crew, including 2 non-RAF members.	204 RAF
28-11-1942	W6016 – Aircraft went missing at 23.45. 14 crew presumed killed. En route to Gibraltar.	204 RAF
22-02-1943	????? – 07.15 – Starboard inner burst into flames 8 miles off Plymouth. Landed successfully.	461 RAAF
02-03-1943	W3979 – 12.30 – Unable to land at base due bad weather; diverted, but had to force land near St. Govan's Head. Pembs. injuring 2 crew. Taken in tow by trawler, but subsequently sunk by RN destroyer.	10 RAAF
02-03-1943	W3983 – Forced landing due to poor weather & lack of fuel.	10 RAAF
20-05-1943	W3986 – 05.20, Caught fire 25 minutes after take-off & crashed 4 miles NW of Eddystone light house.	10 RAAF
07-10-1943	W3993 – 05.10, Hit buoy on take-off for patrol.	10 RAAF
18-10-1943	DD865 – 23.00, Struck mooring buoy while taxying for Ops. In Plymouth Sound	10 RAAF
11-11-1943	EK573 – 09.48, Forced landing safely in Scillies after starboard inner propeller flew off while on anti-sub. patrol.	10 RAAF
30-11-1943	DV989 – 05.00, Struck obstruction while taxying for T/O for Ops.	461 RAF
14-12-1943	W4024 – Landed heavily soon after take-off for Ops. Pilot not in full aileron control.	10 RAAF
30-01-1944	DD865 – 15.47, Struck obstruction while taxying after landing from anti-sub. patrol.	10 RAAF
01-06-1944	EK574 – Taxying for take-off for anti-sub. patrol when aircraft struck buoy & sank. Crew escaped.	10 RAAF
30-06-1944	EK586 – 05.20, Couldn't get enough speed up for take-off for ops. Tail struck waves heavily.	10 RAAF
04-07-1944	DD852 – Drifted onto rock ledge while taxying, prior to anti-sub. patrol.	10 RAAF

Date:	Aircraft & Details:	Squadron:
17-07-1944	DD852 – 13.20, Struck submerged object while taxying in Plymouth Sound prior to test flight.	10 RAAF
16-09-1944	EK573 – 17.40, Ditched after starboard outer caught fire while on ops.	10 RAAF
24-10-1944	NJ253 – 11.30, Drifted ashore while taxying to buoy.	10 RAAF
15-11-1944	ML830 – 01.55, Flares jammed in chute while on Radar and flare exercise: flare ignited but extinguished.	10 RAAF
11-12-1944	ML828 – 13.00, Starboard float damaged on landing in heavy swell.	10 RAAF
19-01-1945	NJ256 – 10.20, Collided with Catalina JKX428 after losing power from port outer engine while taxying for take-off for ops.	10 RAAF
14-02-1945	ML828 – 06.15, Struck Sunderland PP142, whilst taxying for take-off in poor visibility	10 RAAF
16-04-1945	NJ253 – 04.45, Moored, hit by Sunderland NJ254	10 RAAF
16-04-1945	NJ254 – 04.45, Hit Sunderland NJ253 while taxying for ops.	10 RAAF
07-05-1945	ML848 – 14.00, Hit ballon cable over Plymouth Sound while on training flight. Landed safely.	10 RAAF

FINIS

Signed, Vic Hodgkinson 2002

Postscript

During his RAAF service in Australia, Vic Hodgkinson's flying log records that he also briefly flew German Dornier Do 24 flying boats which had been evacuated from the Dutch East Indies (Indonesia).

He remained a pilot for the remainder of his working life, settling in the UK. He flew the Short Sandringham and Plymouth, the de Havilland Comet airliner, Canadair CL-4 Argonaut (Douglas DC-4), Bristol Britannia, and Boeing 707, all for BOAC.

Vic Hodgkinson retired from BOAC in 1971. In his retirement, refurbished the Short Sandringham, *Beachcomber*, currently in Southampton's excellent Solent Sky Museum, where he is commemorated.

He lived in Lymington, Hampshire, and passed away in 2010. His ashes are interred in St. Thomas's churchyard there. He left three sons and eight

Self with my grandsons, David (currently a Captain with British Airways), on the left, and Sam (currently a Squadron Leader with the RAF, flying Chinook helicopters) in 2004.

Vic's grave marker in St Thomas's Churchyard, Lymington, Hampshire. He was a Captain for BOAC and a Wing Commander with the RAAF, hence the dual ranks.

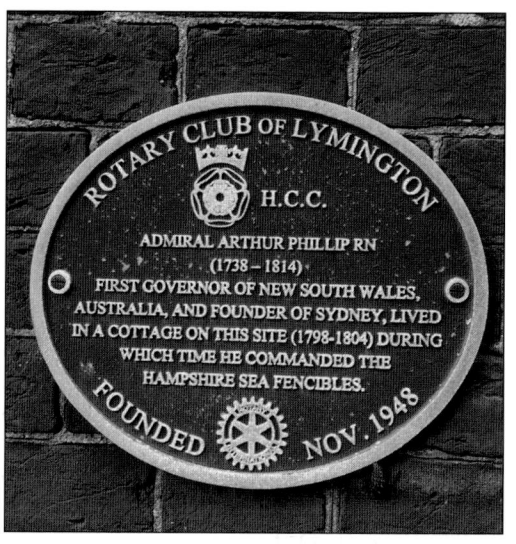

Lymington was also, at one time, the home of Admiral Arthur Phillip, the first governor of New South Wales.

grandchildren; his two grandsons are currently both pilots. David, a Captain with British Airways, and Sam, initially with the Royal Navy, has since transferred to the Royal Air Force, in which he is currently a Squadron Leader.

The photographs included here are a small selection from Vic Hodgkinson's photo albums. From 1798 to 1803 Lymington was also the home to Admiral Arthur Phillip, 1st Governor of New South Wales.

In commemoration of Wing Commander "Vic" Hodgkinson DFC MID,
Royal Australian Air Force, 1916 – 2010,
who spent many happy hours refurbishing "Beachcomber".

During his flying career, "Vic" flew over 7,200 hours
in a variety of British, American and German flying boats, including:
Consolidated Catalina (PBY-5 & PB2B-2), de Havilland DH.60 Floatplane,
Dornier Do 24, Douglas Dolphin, Martin Mariner, Short Singapore,
Short Sunderland (Marks I, II & III), Supermarine Seagull V/Walrus
and Supermarine Scapa.
During the Second World War he served in the Atlantic, Mediterranean
and Pacific theatres and when serving with 10 Squadron RAAF in the UK,
he flew from Calshot, Plymouth, Pembroke Dock and Oban.

Index

Aeroplane magazine, 223
Aircraft;
    Arado floatplane, 154
    Avro Anson, 6–7, 10
    Avro Avian, 1
    Avro Cadet 643, 23
    Avro Lancastrian, 224–5
    Avro Tudor 225
    Avro Tutor, 21, 23–4
    Avro York, 225
    Besson MB.411, 102
    Black Cats, 205
    Blackburn (Sunderlands), 158
    Boeing 707, 223, 228, 235
    Boeing B-24, Liberator, 217
    Boeing Stratocruiser, 225
    Bristol Beaufighters, 168
    Bristol Beaufort, 164, 193
    Bristol Blenheim, 103
    Bristol Britannia, 227, 235
    Canadair CL-4 Argonaut, 226, 235
    Consolidated Catalina, 22, 60, 166, 171–87, 192, 194–5, 203–205, 208, 211, 221–3
    Consolidated B-24 Liberator, 217
    Douglas C-47 Dakota, 217
    de Havilland Comet, 227–8, 235
    de Havilland Tiger Moth, 44
    de Havilland 60 Moth, 21–2, 24, 42, 44
    de Havilland Gipsy Moth, 210
    de Havilland 60 Moth Floatplane, 37–8, 42–3
    de Havilland 86, 2
    Dornier Do 24, 219, 235
    Douglas Dolphin, 189–90
    Fairey 111D Floatplane, 40
    Fairey Swordfish, 152
    Focke-Wulf 200 Condor, 154–7
    Fokker *Southern Cross* 1
    Junkers Ju 88, 154, 163–4
    Hawker Demon, 5-6
    Heinkel He115 float plane, 125, 144
    Lockheed Altair, 1
    Lockheed Constellation, 225
    Lockheed Hudson A28/9, 195
    Martin Mariner PBM-1, 189, 191
    Messerschmitt Bf 110, 153
    Miles Magister, 24
    Mitsubishi Zero, 195
    Saro Lerwick, 53
    Saro London, 157–8
    Short flying boats;
    Short Empire C Class flying boat, 46, 209, 213;
        Carpenteria, 45
        Clare, 91
    Short Empire G Class flying boat, *Golden Fleece,* 144
    Short Hythe, 224–5
    Short Plymouth, 235
    Short Sandringham, *Beachcomber,* 212–13, 225, 229, 235
    Short Solent, 225
    Short Singapore, 52–9
    Short Sunderland, 60–5, 70–85, 94–7, 111–14, 121–4, 127, 147–8, 156, 162, 166–7, 175–6, 212–16, 218, 222
    Short Sunderland interiors, 73–80, 97, 149, 166
    Short Sunderland *Islander,* 121, 212
    Short Sunderland launching, 82–4
    Supermarine Scapa, 52, 54
    Supermarine Seagull V/Walrus, 8, 10, 37, 41–4, 46–51, 74, 77, 98, 174, 203, 205–207
    Supermarine Southampton, 15–16, 37, 39, 60
    Vought-Sikorsky OS2U Kingfisher, 174
    Westland Wapiti, 20–1, 24–5, 30–4, 36
Albatross, HMAS (seaplane tender), 8

Aircraft Construction Course, 1
Aircraft Depot, No. 2, 8
Air Force Law, 19
Air to Surface Vessel Radar (ASV), 87, 101, 133
Air Service Training (Hamble), 224
Aldis Lamp, 91, 120–1, 123, 128, 131, 145, 161
Alexandria, 104–106, 145–8, 152, 168, 224
Altimeter, 142
Amos, Corporal Cliff (RAAF), 131, 134, 144
Angle Bay (Pembroke), 163
Ansett Airways, 211
Appendix, 230
Armament, 31, 46, 73, 78, 126, 150, 155–6, 161, 167, 170, 178–84, 205, Torpedoes 193–4
Atlantis (ship), 163
Australian Commandos, 200
Australian Division, 7th, 196
Australia House (London), 51

Ballali (Solomons), 199
Bay of Biscay, 154, 159
Bell, Flight Lieutenant (RAAF), 74
Bell, Leading Aircraftsman, Ralph (RAAF), 131, 144
Bennet Don, Air Vice Marshall (RAF), 226
Benno (ship), 163
Berlindra (ship), 161–2
Bismarck Sea (battle), 199–200
Blackburns, 158, 166
BOAC, 164, 222–6, 229–30, 235
Bomber Command Pathfinder Force, (RAF), 226
Bowen, 188
Bradbury, Flight Sergeant (RAF), 131, 134–5, 138–9, 143
Broken, Bay, 205
Bristol Hotel (Gibraltar), 159
British Airways, 231
British South American Airways, (BSAA) 226–7
Buka Passage, 189
Burns Philp & Co, 207
Busirus (ship), 135, 137

Cadet Sergeant, 28–9
Cadet Pilot Training, 2
Canada, Vichy French hospital ship, 152
Chapman, Squadron Leader 'Chappie' (RAAF), 198
Chief Flying Instructor (Point Cook), 21
Chichester, Francis, 210
Citizens Air Force (RAAFVR), 66
Coast Watchers, 196–7, 200
Commandos, Australian, 200
Convoy HX, 54, 96
Corcoran, Corporal (RAAF), 131, 134, 143–4
Costello, Flying Officer John, Red Jack (RAAF),124
Court of Enquiry, 141
Courtney, Flight Lieutenant, Bruce, (RAAF), 117
Cox, Flight Engineer Bobby (RAAF), 183
Cunningham, Admiral, 150–1

'Dagwood' (my Catalina), 192
Darcey, Sergeant (RAAF), 182
De Gaulle, family rescue, 74–7
DFC (Distinguished Flying Cross), 201–202
Dönitz, Grand Admiral, 167
Dragon Service, 224
Drogues, 175
Duke of Kent, 104
Duke of Windsor, 93

Engines;
   Bristol Pegasus engines, 100, 127, 165, 167
   Bristol Proteus engines, 227
   Pratt & Whitney engines 100, 165, 167, 174, 177, 228
   Rolls Royce Merlin 626, 226
   Rolls-Royce Conway engines, 228
Egerton, 2nd Flight Sergeant Tom (RAAF), 131, 134
Empire Air Training Scheme, 29, 68
Esplanade Hotel (Oban), 120

Fantasy of Flight Museum (Polk City), 212
Flare Path, 102, 112, 186

Flare Path officer (Pembroke Dock), 141
Food, 26–7
Francis, Armourer John (RAAF), 131, 144
Fugleman, 26
Furner (née. Wearne), Penny, 172, 206
   see also Wearne, Athol

Galdhouro Island, 150
Garing, Captain (RAAF), 104
Gasmata, 194, 199–200
Geffen, Colin van, 60–1
Gehrig, Sergeant Con (RAAF), 131, 134, 143–4
Gibraltar, 103–104, 145, 158–60
Gillies, Ron (RAAF), 90, 121
Glenorchy (ship), 168, 170
Gneisenau, (battleship), 130
Goble, Air Vice Marshall (RAAF), 36
Goldberg, Admiral, 151
Goodenough Island, 201
Gort, Lord, Allied Commander in Chief, 90
Gremlins, 185
Ground Effect, 186
Guernsey, St. Peter Port, 55–9

Haile Selassie, 93
Harris, Sergeant (RAAF), 74
Hazard, Jacques (Free French pilot), 102–103
Hemsworth, Flight Lieutenant (RAAF), 195–6
Hewitt, Corporal Francis (RAAF), 131, 144
HMS *Hood*, 85
HMS *Newcastle*, 98
HMS *Truant*, 107
HMS *Vanoc*, 164
Hodgkinson, Senior First Officer David (BA), 230–1
Hodgkinson, Frank, 196
Hodgkinson, Roy, 196
Hodgkinson, Squadron Leader Sam (RAF), 230–1
Holyhead Sailors Hospital, 137–41
Hong Kong, 224–5

Imperial Airways, 91, 223–4
Imperial Hotel (Cairns), 188

Isle of Sark (ship), 59
Isle of Wight (Saro), 159

Janna (ship), 96
Jervis Bay, 192
Johannesburg, 225
Joyce, Flying Officer Tom (RAAF), 131, 134, 143–4

Kalafrana, 105, 158
Kahili (Solomon Islands), 199
Kererra (Isle of), 113
Kingsford Smith, Charles, 1
Knox-Knight, Wing Commander (RAAF), 122, 125
Kokoda Trail, 195–6

Lae, 189, 199
Laverack, Lieutenant General John, 201
Lake Biscarosse, 89–93
Lake Macquarie (Rathmines), 205
Laurentic, (ship), 110
Lee-on-Solent, 229
Leningrad, 228
Lloyd George, Lord David, 89–93
Loan Flights, 221
London Illustrated News, 117
Lord Howe Island, 203, 207–11
Lord Gort, John, *see* Gort, Lord, Allied Commander in Chief
Lukis, Group Captain, Francis 'Frank' (RAAF), 36
Lush, Flight Lieutenant 'Ginty' (RAAF), 126
Lymington (UK), 229, 231

Maintenance of aircraft, 69–70, 99, 101
Maintenance Units,
   No 1 Flying Boat (Lake Boga), 205
Malta, 104–105, 145–6, 158
Mandang, 213
Marriage (to Teresa Myers), 168–9
Martin, Flying Officer (RAAF), 144
Mascot (Kingsford Smith airport), 2, 8
Maxaret anti-skid braking, 227
Menzies, Australian Prime Minister Sir Robert, 69

Middleton Reef (Lord Howe Island), 203
'Milk Runs', 193, 195–6, 199, 201
Mitchell, R.J., 207
Moscow, 228
Moss Hutchinson Line, 137

National Heritage Memorial Trust, 229
Navigators, 10 Squadron, 70
Navigation;
　Browns Table for Navigation, 32
　Navigation Calculator, 32
New Britain, 194
New Guinea, 189, 195
No. 2 Aircraft Depot, 8
No. 11 Seaplane Conversion Course, 9, 37, 39

Oban (Scotland), 110–25
Ole Jacob (ship), 163
Orion (ship), 164

Panama Canal, 170
Pan American Airways, 92
Pantelleria, 153
Parachutes, 143
Parachute training, 14–15
Park Hotel (Oban, Scotland), 111
Passing Out Parade, 35–6
Phillip, Admiral, Arthur (RN), 236
Pigeons, 136 (with Vic), 164–5
Podger, Flight Lieutenant, Ian, (RAAF), 115, 117
Poole (UK), 164, 223
Port Moresby (New Guinea), 213–15
Port Stevens (Australia), 205
Postscript, 225
Pwllheli Borough Cemetery (Wales, UK), 144

QANTAS Airways, 45, 196, 205, 207, 211–12, 219

RAAF Headquarters (Melbourne), 171
RAAF Headquarters, Eastern Area, Sydney, 221–2
RAAF Overseas HQ (London, Kodak House), 167

RAAF Squadrons;
　No 3, 66
　No 9, 205
　No 10, 45, 70 (Navigators), 71, 94–5, 188
　No 11, 188
　No 20, 187–8, 200–202, 204
　No 40, 71, 191, 213, 218–19
　No 461, 164
RAAF Staff School, Mount Martha (Melbourne), 219–20
RAAF Stations/Bases;
　Bowen, 188, 193, 199
　Cairns, 188–90, 193, 201
　Lake Boga, 189, 205
　Milne Bay, 195, 197, 199
　Mount Martha (Melbourne), 219–20
　Nowra, 193, 205
　Point Cook (Flying Training School), 11–12, 24, 35, 220–2
　Rathmines, No. 3 Operational Training Unit (OTU), 171–3, 187, 202, 204–207, 209, 222
　Richmond, 1–2, 6
　Townsville, 213–17
RAAFVR (Australian Citizens Air Force), 66
RAF Bases (UK);
　Boscombe Down, 167
　Bowmore (Isle of Islay), 128
　Calshot, 51–61
　Invergordon 121–3, 142
　Mount Batten (Plymouth), 69, 81–8, 145, 156–9
　Oban, 110–30
　Pembroke Dock, 62–8, 129, 131
RAF Museum, Hendon (UK), 48, 206
RAF Squadrons;
　No. 202, 158
　No. 210, 62–4, 110
　No. 230, 64, 147–8, 153
Radar, Air to Surface Vessel (ASV), 87, 101, 133
Raine, Leading Aircraftman Norman (RAAF), 131, 144
Runnymede Memorial, 144
Rose Bay (Sydney), 205, 207, 209–10, 212

Salamau, 189
Saro works (Cowes), 159

Index

Scharnhorst, battleship, 130
Science Museum, 229
Sercombe, Pilot Officer (RAF), 124
'Shags' (Pigeon), 134–6, 138
Short Brothers, 165–7
Singapore, 168, 224
Smith, Squadron Leader (RAAF), 218
Solent Sky Museum/Hall of Aviation (Southampton), 212–13, 229, 235
Southampton City Council, 229
Sperry auto pilot, 178
Squadron Leader (promotion to), 192
Stirling Castle, 223
Sumba, 193
Surcouf (French submarine), 102
St. Peter Port, Guernsey, 55–9
Stanngrant (ship,) 115–19
Station Radio Officer (Pembroke Dock), 141
Supply Drop Operations, 196
Sugar bowl (incident of…), 96
Sumba, 193
Sydney Morning Herald, 223
Sydney Technical College, 1

Tasman Empire Air Services (TEAL), 209
Thurstun, Flying Officer Gilbert 'Thursty' (RAAF), 12, 37, 39, 104, 115, 124, 168
Torpedoes (Catalina), 193–4
Trobriand Islands, 200–201
Tropic Sea (ship), 107

U Boat (half of…), 129
U34, 96
U37, 115–16
Uniform, 9–10, 13, 16, 19, 26, 67, 137
United States Army Air Force (USAAF), 183
USS *Jarvis,* 189

Vernon, Flying Officer Dave, (RAAF), 126, 128
Vichy French Destroyer, 152
Vichy French Hospital ship, *Canada,* 152
Victoria Barracks (Melbourne), 217
Vitiaz Strait, 199

Warrant Officer Drill Instructor, 17
Wearne, Flight Lieutenant Athol 'Attie', (RAAF), 12, 29, 37, 39, 107, 120, 132
see also Furner, Penny
'Web Footers Club', 222
Wedding, 167–9
Wellington (New Zealand), 170–1
Whicham (St. Mary) Churchyard, 144
Willams, Air Marshall 'Dickie' (RAAF), 168

Zwicky (hand pump), 159

Dear Reader,

We hope you have enjoyed this book, but why not share your views on social media? You can also follow our pages to see more about our other products: facebook.com/penandswordbooks or follow us on Twitter @penswordbooks

You can also view our products at www.pen-and-sword.co.uk (UK and ROW) or www.penandswordbooks.com (North America).

To keep up to date with our latest releases and online catalogues, please sign up to our newsletter at: www.pen-and-sword.co.uk/newsletter

If you would like a printed catalogue with our latest books, then please email: enquiries@pen-and-sword.co.uk or telephone: 01226 734555 (UK and ROW) or email: Uspen-and-sword@casematepublishers.com or telephone: (610) 853-9131 (North America).

We respect your privacy and we will only use personal information to send you information about our products.

Thank you!